POLICING, EDUCATION, AND THE BENEFITS OF BECOMING A POLICE OFFICER

DR. WINSTON HARRIS

Published in USA by Trinity Publishing Company
Paperback ISBN: 978-1-964707-73-0
Book Cover and Formatting: Trinity Publishing Company
Editing: McKoy Moss

DISCLAIMER

The views and opinions expressed in this book are those of the author and do not necessarily reflect Trinity Publishing Company. Neither does it reflect any official policies or positions of any educational institution, law enforcement agency, or governmental organization. The information presented is intended for educational and informational purposes only and should not be construed as legal or professional advice.

While every effort has been made to ensure the accuracy and reliability of the content, the author acknowledges that the field of higher education and policing is complex and continuously evolving.

The author and publisher disclaim any liability for any direct, indirect, incidental, or consequential damages arising from the use or interpretation of the information contained within this book.

TABLE OF CONTENTS

INTRODUCTION

In the field of law enforcement, where lives and communities are often impacted by split-second decisions, there is an increasing demand for approaches grounded in both comprehensive research and practical application. Police departments worldwide are grappling with complex issues as societal expectations shift, emphasizing accountability, transparency, and empathy. This book examines the diverse factors that contribute to effective policing by comparing elements within U.S. police forces and other countries, including the significance of evidence-based practices, education, empathy, and the growing value of a structured career trajectory. By examining the strategies and practices that support a competent and well-prepared police force, this comparative study aims to uncover best practices that support a more effective, informed, and adaptable policing framework.

One critical component of this study is an exploration of the importance of a 10-year career plan in policing. In both Turkey and the United States, officers benefit from long-term planning and professional development, which help reduce burnout, increase job satisfaction, and improve decision-making under pressure. Policymakers in both countries increasingly advocate for clear career advancement paths, and this study investigates how such frameworks enhance performance, stability, and overall job satisfaction. The study also examines the length of time officers stay in service and how this tenure impacts the overall competency and adaptability of police forces in both countries.

The study further investigates the contrasting approaches to empathy, which plays a critical role in building trust between officers and the communities they serve. In Turkey, where the police force often holds a more centralized and authoritative position, empathy training may differ significantly from U.S.

1

practices, where police departments vary widely across states in their community engagement approaches. Through these comparisons, we gain a better understanding of how empathy can shape policing culture and potentially reduce instances of conflict. This study emphasizes the importance of education and job preparedness for officers. Higher education levels have been linked to improved problem-solving skills, greater understanding of diverse communities, and better handling of high-stress situations. This research evaluates the training and educational qualifications required by both Turkish and U.S. forces and explores how these requirements impact the quality of service provided.

Another focal point of this study is the value of evidence-based policing. In both the Turkish and U.S. forces, there is a growing acknowledgment that factual, data-driven decision-making is superior to intuitive, gut-based policing. While intuition has historically been an important element in policing, the limitations of intuitive approaches are becoming more evident, especially as new technologies enable police forces to analyze data on criminal behavior and community dynamics. This study highlights how evidence-based practices can improve accuracy, enhance accountability, and promote better long-term results. It also discusses the correlation between evidence-based policing and the theory of cognitive development, suggesting that officers who are trained in systematic analysis may be better equipped to make sound decisions in complex, high-stakes environments.

Salary, job stability, and incentives are examined as they relate to the recruitment and retention of officers. Modern policing incentives differ not only within regions in the U.S.—from the East Coast to the West Coast and southern states—but also between countries, particularly when comparing the U.S. to Turkey and other nations like the United Kingdom. Variations in pension plans, salaries, and benefits influence the appeal of policing as a career, and these factors can have long-term effects on workforce stability and officer morale. This analysis explores these variations, tracing their evolution from the

1960s through the 2000s, a period marked by groundbreaking reforms and increased professionalization of the police force.

In addition to these considerations, this study addresses the impact of military experience on policing. Military-trained officers bring unique skills to the field, including discipline and teamwork, but the transition to civilian policing requires a nuanced approach to community engagement. By analyzing this aspect, we gain insight into how military experience both complements and challenges traditional policing frameworks.

Finally, the study places these themes within broader historical and legislative frameworks, such as the Civil Rights Act of 1964 and subsequent reforms, which significantly impacted U.S. policing practices and set the stage for ongoing change. Through the lens of these reforms, the study compares the structures and operational methods, offering a comprehensive understanding of the evolution of policing practices.

In examining these aspects of policing, this study aims to provide a well-rounded view of how various elements—tenure, empathy, education, evidence-based practices, military experience, and incentives—collectively contribute to effective law enforcement. By recognizing both the parallels and distinctions of other countries policing, this study aspires to inform future strategies and encourage dialogue around enhancing police professionalism and public trust on a global scale.

PREFACE

In the evolving landscape of global policing, there is a pressing need to revisit and re-evaluate the factors that influence police effectiveness and community trust. This work was born from the desire to better understand the unique and universal aspects of law enforcement across borders. Drawing upon statistical data, historical context, and comparative analyses, this examination aims to uncover trends and best practices that could enhance modern policing.

Researchers, police officers, and policymakers whose insights made this study possible have provided valuable perspectives on the challenges and opportunities facing law enforcement in an increasingly interconnected world. Their contributions have shed light on the complex dynamics that shape public trust in policing and offer potential solutions for building stronger relationships between law enforcement agencies and the communities they serve.

Their dedication to advancing evidence-based policing and promoting empathy and preparedness within law enforcement continues to shape a brighter, more resilient future for communities worldwide. By focusing on innovative strategies and establishing collaboration between law enforcement and community members, these researchers have paved the way for more effective and sustainable approaches to policing. Their work underscores the importance of ongoing dialogue and cooperation in addressing the evolving needs of society and ensuring public safety for all.

CHAPTER 01

THEN AND NOW ON POLICING

The evolution of policing in the United States mirrors the nation's societal shifts, changes in governance, and drive toward higher standards of justice and accountability. Early law enforcement systems were informal and community-oriented, embodying a different model than the formal police structures we see today. The journey of American policing from loosely organized community efforts to a formalized, professional institution has been a gradual yet transformative one. Beginning with the establishment of the "watch system" in the 1600s, policing evolved through various historical eras, each shaped by the needs and values of the time. These developments reflect the ongoing pursuit of more effective and ethical law enforcement.

The roots of American policing lie in Boston, Massachusetts, where, in the 1630s, local citizens organized night watches to safeguard their communities. These "night watchmen" marked the nation's earliest attempts at structured law enforcement, relying heavily on community participation rather than professional officers. This model spread as other cities recognized the benefits of a communal approach to safety, leading Philadelphia to establish day watches in 1833 and New York to follow suit with its own watch system. Unlike the centralized, professional police forces established in England, the American model was decentralized and community-focused, built around the needs and governance of local populations. Local sheriffs and constables became key figures, responsible for maintaining order in their respective communities.

American law enforcement's foundation in community-oriented watch systems contributed to a unique policing ethos centered on local governance and citizen involvement. These early systems set a precedent for the ways in which police interacted with the public, emphasizing responsiveness to community concerns. This contrasts with the British system, where centralized police forces operated under a national government mandate. The U.S. approach fostered a strong local identity within law enforcement, shaping practices and attitudes that persist in some ways even in today's policing landscape.

As the country's urban centers expanded and populations grew, the limitations of the watch system became more evident, leading to demands for more organized and professional policing. Cities like New York and Philadelphia experienced increased crime and public disorder, necessitating a shift from community watches to professional forces.

In response, police departments began to take on more formal structures yet still maintained a connection to their local communities. This historical context highlights how American policing evolved to meet the changing needs of society, balancing local governance with the need for a more structured law enforcement presence.

American policing today is rooted in this historical progression from night watch patrols to modern professional law enforcement. By tracing these origins, it becomes clear how past methods and philosophies have influenced contemporary policing approaches, particularly in areas such as community relations and decentralized structures. While law enforcement has significantly transformed, the influence of its origins is still present in the ways police agencies engage with local communities and prioritize public trust.

During the turn of the 20th century, August Vollmer was instrumental in advancing policing and higher education. He served as a police chief in Berkeley, California, and led the charge in creating a criminal justice program. This initiative helped elevate the police to a more professional level. After the Wickersham Commission's recommendation, policing and education became the focus of intensive research. It was ground-breaking on so many levels, and scholars and experts recognized the need for well-trained and educated police officers to effectively address the many challenging issues the world was experiencing during this time of crime and social issues. As a result, numerous universities across the United States began offering criminal justice programs, providing aspiring law enforcement professionals with the necessary knowledge and skills to get beyond where policing had been and to evolve the landscape of policing. This emphasis on education marked a significant shift in the approach to law enforcement, fostering a more sophisticated and effective response to crime. Eyes were becoming wide open after this shift, as it became evident that a well-educated and trained police force could better understand the reason many of the crimes were happening. The force addressed the underlying social issues that contributed to the crimes. This new perspective led to a greater emphasis on community policing, proactive crime prevention strategies, and the use of data-driven approaches to target high-crime areas. Questions were being answered about who, what, when, why, and where when it came to the community and what was happening as a whole. Experts wanted to examine college-educated police officers and their performance. It was essential to understand how education could impact the effectiveness of law enforcement. The results of these studies were used to implement changes that would ultimately improve the safety and security of communities. It was very impactful and led to a decrease in crime rates in those targeted areas. The studies were astounding and almost unbelievable.

They highlighted the importance of community engagement and collaboration in creating a safer environment. By involving the community in decision-making processes and establishing trust between law enforcement and residents, a positive relationship was fostered, further enhancing the overall effectiveness of policing strategies. It wasn't an easy approach to get the community leaders and residents on board with this new way of thinking and doing things, but it caught on eventually, and the results were significant. Crime rates decreased, and residents felt safer and more supported by law enforcement. This collaborative approach also led to increased transparency and accountability within the police force as community members became active participants in shaping policies and procedures.

During the 1960s, the President's Commission on Law Enforcement and Administration of Justice recommended that police officers attain a four-year degree in criminal justice before their appointment. This was in response to widespread civil unrest throughout the United States, which had led to public mistrust of the police agencies and concerns about corruption within law enforcement. The Commission hoped that requiring higher education for police officers would help address these issues and promote more positive perceptions of law enforcement among citizens. If the officers had a four-year education in criminal justice, they were more likely to understand the people and the things they would go through from one neighborhood to another. Empathy was another key benefit of higher education for police officers. By studying criminal justice, officers gain a deeper understanding of the community where they are policed and why many of the same crimes are being committed. There was social unrest in many communities, which also contributed to crimes being committed. The officers could better understand, even if they couldn't relate or wrap their minds around how someone could do some of the crimes that were being done; however, they could better empathize with the challenges faced by individuals in different communities. This increased empathy can lead to more effective community policing strategies and improved relationships between law enforcement and the public. Additionally, higher education equips officers with critical thinking and problem-solving skills that are essential for making informed decisions in high-pressure situations, ultimately enhancing their ability to serve and protect their communities.

In the 1970s, there were problems with government funding for criminal justice programs. This led to a decrease in resources available for law enforcement agencies and the development of effective crime prevention strategies.

As a result, the criminal justice system faced challenges in effectively addressing rising crime rates and ensuring public safety. Numerous research studies have discovered a link between police officers with a college education and better performance. These studies have shown that officers with higher education are more likely to exhibit critical thinking skills, problem-solving abilities, and a deeper understanding of legal and ethical issues. Additionally, they tend to have better communication skills, which can help in building trust and fostering positive relationships with the community they serve. An inquiry by Finnegan (1976) found that officers with higher education had better performance evaluation scores when compared to those who had not pursued higher education. They were prepared and equipped, whereas, on the other hand, those who did not pursue a higher education were more likely to make mistakes or have difficulties handling complex situations and problem-solving skills.

Higher education provides officers with a broader perspective and critical thinking skills that are essential for effective decision-making in the field. It also allows them to stay updated with the latest advancements in law enforcement practices and technologies, ensuring they can adapt to the evolving nature of crime and security challenges. It's better to be equipped with knowledge and a good understanding of the world around you than to step outside and face unfamiliar situations without the necessary tools to handle them. Also, higher education can enhance an officer's communication skills, enabling them to effectively interact with diverse communities and diffuse tense situations. By investing in their education, officers are better prepared to protect and serve their communities, creating trust and cooperation between law enforcement and the public. This would be one of the number one reasons why a higher education is vital to a police officer. You should be more than qualified to deal with and handle high-pressure situations and people from all backgrounds.

THE WATCH SYSTEM

The history of policing in the United States begins in Boston, Massachusetts, where local citizens took it upon themselves to patrol their city and ensure the safety of their fellow citizens. These citizen patrols, known as "night watchmen," were established in the 1630s and marked the earliest form of organized law enforcement in the country. As the colonies grew, so did the need for more formalized policing systems, leading to the creation of the first official police force in Boston in 1838. In the early 19th century, the American law enforcement system differed from England's centralized and authoritarian system. Instead, it adopted a decentralized and community-oriented approach, with local sheriffs and constables playing key roles in maintaining law and order.

This emphasis on community involvement and cooperation continues to be a defining characteristic of the American law enforcement system today. Homelessness, addiction, and being a good neighbor to the community are ways that policing has evolved since the 1800s.

Philadelphia introduced first-day watch patrols in 1833, which New York later adopted to improve policing in urban areas. These patrols consisted of officers patrolling the streets during the day and night, responding to calls for assistance, and preventing crime. This innovation marked a significant shift towards a more proactive and visible presence of law enforcement in cities, setting the stage for modern policing strategies. As political influence over the police grew, there was a push for reform and consideration of alternative leadership options. One of the proposed alternatives was the establishment of civilian oversight boards, which aimed to provide community input and accountability in policing decisions. There was also a growing recognition of the need for specialized units within police departments to address specific issues such as drug enforcement and community relations. They often get to know the people in the area, and it works both ways because the residents become friendly with some of the officers and can trust them in many ways. This is supposed to be a win-win situation for all involved. Especially when the specialized units can foster a sense of familiarity and trust between officers and community members, leading to more effective crime prevention and resolution. By building relationships and understanding the unique needs of the community, officers can tailor their approach to better serve and protect the residents they serve. This collaborative effort ultimately strengthens the overall safety and well-being of the community.

POLITICAL ERA

From 1840 to 1930, local politicians appointed police chiefs of municipal and county departments. This system only led to corruption and favoritism within the police force, as politicians would choose individuals based on personal connections rather than merit. During this era, police chiefs had little power over their officers, which caused widespread corruption and favoritism between politicians and patrol officers (Stevens, 2017). The lack of accountability and professionalism within law enforcement agencies during this era had detrimental effects on the public's trust and safety. The corruption and favoritism that resulted from politicians' personal connections further eroded the integrity of the police force, hindering its ability to effectively serve and protect communities. Some corrupt activities stemming from politicians' abuse of authority include police officers' poor decisions, such as engaging in illegal activities themselves or turning a blind eye to criminal behavior in exchange for personal favors.

This compromised the fairness and impartiality of law enforcement, leaving communities vulnerable to crime and injustice. The lack of consequences for these unethical actions created a culture of impunity within the police force, further perpetuating corruption and eroding public trust. Some of the officers turned in false reports that falsely accused innocent individuals of crimes they did not commit. This not only tarnished the reputation of the victims but also resulted in wrongful convictions and a miscarriage of justice. These deceitful practices undermined the credibility of the entire justice system, making it difficult for communities to have faith in the police's ability to protect and serve them. There was also poor training (Stevens, 2017). The lack of proper training further exacerbated the issue, as it failed to equip officers with the necessary skills and knowledge to handle situations ethically and responsibly. This created a breeding ground for misconduct and abuse of power within law enforcement, further eroding public trust in their ability to uphold justice.

Concern about the political influence of policing operations led President Herbert Hoover to appoint General George Wickersham to oversee the Commission on Law Observance and Enforcement, which was responsible for reforming the police profession (Stevens, 2017).

COMMISSION ON LAW

Observance and Enforcement, also known as the Wickersham Commission, conducted a comprehensive study of law enforcement practices and made recommendations for improvement. One of the key findings was the need for standardized training and education for police officers to ensure they possess the necessary skills and knowledge to handle situations ethically and responsibly. If they don't receive proper training, there could be a higher risk of misconduct and abuse of power. The Wickersham Commission's recommendations led to the establishment of police academies and the development of a standardized curriculum to address this issue. This marked a significant step towards addressing the issues of misconduct and abuse of power within law enforcement, ultimately aiming to rebuild public trust in their ability to uphold justice.

REFORM ERA

Back in 1931, the Wickersham Commission discovered that police corruption had a harmful impact, and citizens were worried about the political influence that politicians and police had. The commission's findings prompted calls for reform and stricter oversight of law enforcement agencies.

Many advocated for the establishment of independent bodies to investigate allegations of corruption and ensure accountability within the police force. The citizens demanded transparency in the relationship between politicians and police, pushing for measures to limit undue influence and prevent abuse of power. The crimes committed included extortion, gambling, and conspiring with prostitution. These crimes highlighted the urgent need for comprehensive training programs and ethical guidelines for law enforcement officers. There was a growing demand for increased community engagement and collaboration to rebuild trust between the police and the public in which they served. In 1913, a commission was created in New York City to tackle the lawlessness of police officers nationwide. This commission continued its investigation, publishing its findings in 1930 and 1931 (DOJ, 1990).

In response to the corruption among law enforcement officers, police leaders, and politicians created laws and policies to make policing more professional. These efforts included implementing standardized training programs, establishing professional codes of conduct, and promoting accountability through internal affairs units. Community policing strategies were introduced to encourage closer relationships between police officers and the communities they served. These initiatives aimed to rebuild trust by involving community members in decision-making processes and encouraging collaboration in problem-solving efforts. However, it is important to recognize that rebuilding trust is an ongoing process that requires continuous efforts from both the police and the public.

PROFESSIONALISM

At the turn of the century, there was a pivotal moment in American policing when criminal justice administrators and politicians suggested professionalizing the field. This led to the establishment of the first criminal justice curriculum at the California University of Berkeley by August Vollmer. San Jose Community College also began offering a two-year degree program to educate police officers with a broader perspective to serve citizens better (Finckenauer, 2005). This shift towards professionalization aimed to address the growing complexities of crime and the need for a more systematic approach to law enforcement. By introducing formal education and training programs, administrators and politicians hoped to equip police officers with the necessary skills and knowledge to effectively handle modern challenges in policing. These initiatives marked a significant step towards elevating the standards of American policing and promoting a more professional and accountable approach to law enforcement.

An attempt to enhance professionalism in policing was made through the Minnesota Experience (Carter, 1995). The Minnesota Experience aimed to provide police officers with comprehensive training in areas such as community policing, de-escalation techniques, and cultural sensitivity. This program emphasized the importance of building trust and positive relationships between law enforcement and the communities they serve. The researchers carefully examined and evaluated the misconduct in policing, the impact of politics, and increased remuneration (Carter, 1995). The findings of the Minnesota Experience highlighted the need for ongoing training and education for police officers to address issues such as bias, use of force, and accountability. It also emphasized the role of leadership in implementing effective policies and procedures within law enforcement agencies.

Overall, the program aimed to create a more professional and accountable police force that prioritizes community engagement and trust-building. As a result of the Wickersham report and the Minnesota Experience study, a better understanding of the repercussions of lower education and performance among police officers was achieved. These studies highlighted the importance of education and training in shaping the behavior and decision-making of police officers. They revealed that officers with higher levels of education are more likely to exhibit professionalism, critical thinking skills, and empathy towards the communities they serve. The studies emphasized the need for ongoing performance evaluations and continuous training to ensure that officers maintain a high standard of conduct throughout their careers.

CHAPTER 02

POLICING FROM THE 1960s TO NOW

The landscape of policing incentives and conditions has evolved significantly from the 1960s to today, influenced by social movements, legislation, and societal needs. During the 1960s and 1970s, police officers were attracted to moderate salaries, job stability, and defined benefit pensions that offered financial security after retirement. Policing held social prestige as a respected position within communities. However, this period also marked the Civil Rights Movement, which exposed police brutality and racial discrimination. Key legislative changes, such as the establishment of Miranda Rights in 1966, and the initiation of the War on Drugs under President Nixon, increased funding for drug enforcement and influenced policing strategies.

Policing from the 1960s to the present has been shaped by a combination of legislative changes, societal movements, and evolving public expectations, with each era bringing new challenges and opportunities. The 1960s and 1970s were marked by significant social upheaval, including the Civil Rights Movement, which demanded greater accountability for law enforcement, especially in regard to the treatment of African Americans and other marginalized groups. During this period, police forces across the country were often criticized for their aggressive tactics, which were used to suppress civil rights activists and protests. This period also saw the landmark Supreme Court decision in 1966 that established the Miranda Rights, ensuring that suspects were informed of their right to remain silent and to have legal representation during interrogations. These events set the stage for a wave of legislative reforms that would change how police operated in the years to come.

President Nixon believed that law and order were essential for maintaining social stability, leading to a shift towards more aggressive policing tactics. These changes ultimately shaped the modern landscape of law enforcement in the United States. It was during his tenure that the concept of community policing began to gain traction as a way to improve relations between law enforcement and the communities they serve. The establishment of the Law Enforcement Assistance Administration in 1968 provided resources for police training and equipment, further shaping the future of policing in America.

The War on Drugs, initiated by President Richard Nixon in the 1970s and intensified in the 1980s, had a profound impact on policing. This campaign focused on the criminalization of drug use and distribution, resulting in increased law enforcement efforts aimed at combatting drug-related crimes. Federal and state governments poured significant resources into policing drug offenses, often leading to more aggressive tactics, including militarized responses to drug dealers and drug users, particularly in poor urban areas. The War on Drugs also contributed to mass incarceration, disproportionately affecting minority communities. The funding for drug enforcement agencies increased, and by the 1980s, many police departments were acquiring more military-grade equipment. This era also saw the rise of drug task forces and specialized units within police departments, such as narcotics squads, further shaping the role of law enforcement in American society.

From the 1980s through the early 2000s, the War on Drugs continued to drive funding and aggressive policing tactics, while community policing emerged as a strategy to foster trust between officers and community members. Police unions gained power during this time, securing better pay, benefits, and working conditions for officers. However, this era has also seen public scrutiny rise, with high-profile cases of police misconduct sparking widespread protests and movements like Black Lives Matter. Legislative reforms, including body camera mandates and restrictions on chokeholds, were introduced to increase transparency and accountability.

Throughout the 1980s and into the 1990s, police unions began gaining more influence, fighting for better working conditions, salaries, and job security. Police officers enjoyed increased job stability and were given higher wages in many areas, although the pay remained modest compared to other professions requiring similar levels of training. During this period, pensions remained a critical benefit for officers, and their bargaining power increased as unions advocated for more benefits. The introduction of community policing in the 1990s marked a significant shift in how law enforcement engaged with the public. Rather than relying solely on punitive measures, community policing focused on building stronger relationships between officers and the communities they served. This method aimed to reduce crime through collaboration and preventive strategies rather than aggressive enforcement alone.

By the early 2000s, policing had entered a new phase marked by technological advancements and the rise of surveillance methods. The introduction of body cameras, predictive policing algorithms, and more sophisticated data analytics revolutionized how officers were trained and how policing operations were conducted. These advancements allowed for greater transparency and accountability in law enforcement practices, but they also sparked debates about privacy, the potential for surveillance abuse, and the effectiveness of technology in solving crimes. At the same time, modern incentives for joining the police force began to evolve. Salaries increased significantly, with the average annual salary for police officers rising to around $67,000 by 2023. Cities like California, New York, and Massachusetts offered even higher salaries, with benefits packages that included extensive health insurance, paid leave, and robust pension plans. The opportunity for career advancement, specialized roles, and overtime pay further attracted individuals to law enforcement careers.

The combination of modern incentives and societal pressures on policing has shaped both public perceptions and the effectiveness of law enforcement in addressing contemporary issues. High-profile cases of police misconduct, such as the deaths of individuals like George Floyd, sparked widespread protests and movements like Black Lives Matter. These movements have pushed for legislative changes aimed at reforming police practices, including the use of body cameras, restrictions on chokeholds, and new measures designed to promote accountability and transparency. Public scrutiny and the demand for police reform have led to changes in how officers are trained and the tools available to them. Today's police officers are expected to not only enforce the law but also engage in community relations and uphold the principles of justice and fairness.

Pension plans remain an important incentive, with defined benefit pensions still common, although some regions have shifted toward defined contribution plans. California, for instance, continues to provide generous pensions through CalPERS.

Modern incentives for joining the police force are robust, encompassing competitive salaries, comprehensive benefits, defined benefit pension plans, job stability, career advancement opportunities, and specialized roles. The role also offers the chance to make a meaningful community impact, which is a strong motivator for many. The field's increasing reliance on advanced technology and support from influential police unions further enhances the appeal of a law enforcement career.

Across the U.S., incentives and conditions vary by region. On the East Coast, states like New York and Massachusetts provide high starting salaries, strong pension plans, and powerful unions. On the West Coast, California offers some of the nation's highest salaries, generous pensions, and powerful unions, while Oregon and Washington feature competitive salaries and defined benefit pension plans. In the Southern states, Texas, Florida, and North Carolina show variations in salaries, pension plans, and union strength, with generally lower salaries and less union influence in North Carolina compared to Texas and Florida.

Internationally, police in the United States generally earn higher salaries than those in the United Kingdom. Both countries offer defined benefit pension plans, though the UK has implemented reforms to its pension schemes. U.S. police unions are more influential, often advocating for better conditions and protections for officers. While job stability is high in both countries, budget cuts have occasionally affected police in the UK. Community policing is a central focus in the UK, and public perception is generally positive, contrasting with the varied public perception of police in the U.S., where certain areas experience high public scrutiny. Technological advancements are prominent in both countries; however, U.S. police have greater access to military-grade equipment, while the UK prioritizes less-lethal options and de-escalation techniques. Training and professional development are also structured differently, with national standards and continuous development emphasized in the UK, while U.S. training varies by state and department.

Also, internationally, the comparison between policing in the United States and other countries like the United Kingdom highlights significant differences in both practice and public perception. While U.S. officers are often equipped with military-grade equipment, the UK emphasizes de-escalation techniques and less-lethal options. Additionally, U.S. police unions wield significant influence, often resisting reforms and advocating for the protection of officers' rights, such as qualified immunity. In contrast, the UK's police forces operate with less union influence and a greater focus on accountability. The salaries for law enforcement in the U.S. are generally higher than those in the UK, with U.S. officers enjoying larger pension plans, though the UK's pension system has undergone significant reforms in recent years. Both countries face public scrutiny over police conduct, but the structure and approach to law enforcement vary significantly, with each system shaped by its unique political, social, and economic factors. These international differences reflect the ongoing debate about the role of law enforcement in society and the most effective ways to ensure that police forces serve and protect their communities in a fair and just manner.

Overall, policing incentives have improved over the decades, but differences across the East Coast, West Coast, Southern states, and between countries reflect the influence of local factors such as cost of living, union power, and political climate. Despite challenges, policing remains an attractive career due to financial rewards, job security, and the opportunity to serve the community. Taking all these factors into account can help prospective officers determine which location aligns best with their career goals and personal values.

CHAPTER 03

STATE THE FACTS, MA'AM: THE IMPORTANCE OF EVIDENCE-BASED POLICING OVER INTUITION

In the complex and often contentious world of law enforcement, the methods and approaches used by police officers are under constant scrutiny. Among the various strategies employed, two distinct paradigms often come into focus: evidence-based policing, which emphasizes the reliance on empirical data and factual evidence, and intuitive policing, which involves decisions based on gut feelings and instinct. This chapter explores the critical importance of grounding policing practices in facts and evidence rather than relying on intuition, highlighting the benefits of this approach in enhancing public safety, accountability, and community trust.

It is increasingly important for police officers to receive a college education and training in fairness, empathy, and compassion. A well-rounded education equips officers with critical thinking skills, a deeper understanding of social dynamics, and the ability to analyze complex situations objectively. Training in fairness, empathy, and compassion ensures that officers can approach their duties with an awareness of the diverse communities they serve, fostering stronger relationships and trust.

Relying on intuition or gut feelings, without the foundation of evidence-based practice, can lead to biases and misjudgments that undermine the effectiveness and credibility of law enforcement. By focusing on evidence, officers are better equipped to make informed decisions that align with legal standards and ethical guidelines, reducing the likelihood of wrongful convictions and the erosion of public trust.

Education and training play a major role in shaping competent, fair, and compassionate police officers who prioritize facts and evidence in their work. A college education provides officers with a broad perspective on societal issues, critical thinking skills, and the ability to analyze situations from multiple angles. This educational foundation enables officers to understand the complexities of the communities they serve, resulting in more effective communication and interaction. Training in fairness, empathy, and compassion is equally crucial, as it equips officers with the skills needed to navigate diverse social landscapes and build trust within communities. By emphasizing evidence-based practices over intuition, officers are more likely to make decisions that are objective, fair, and just, reducing the potential for biases and errors. This approach not only enhances the legitimacy of law enforcement but also strengthens community trust and cooperation, ultimately leading to more effective policing and safer communities.

Officers are better equipped to handle the difficulties of modern policing thanks to education and training, which ensures that their decisions are based on facts and evidence rather than instincts or assumptions.

THE ROLE OF FACTS IN POLICING

Understanding Evidence-Based Policing

Evidence-based policing (EBP) is a methodology that prioritizes the use of scientific research and empirical evidence to guide law enforcement strategies, policies, and practices. EBP, created by criminologist Lawrence Sherman in the late 1990s, promotes the incorporation of research findings into decision-making processes to increase the effectiveness and efficiency of policing efforts.

Key components of evidence-based policing include:

- Data Collection and Analysis: Gathering and analyzing crime data to identify patterns and trends.

- Research-Driven Strategies: Implementing strategies proven effective through rigorous research.

- Continuous Evaluation: Assessing the outcomes of policing interventions to refine and improve practices.

The Limitations of Intuitive Policing

While intuition can play a role in certain situations, relying solely on gut feelings in policing poses significant risks. Intuitive policing often leads to biased decision-making, as personal beliefs, stereotypes, and cognitive biases can cloud judgment. This approach can result in unfair treatment, wrongful arrests, and strained community relations.

THE BENEFITS OF EVIDENCE-BASED POLICING

Improved Decision-Making

One of the most significant advantages of evidence-based policing is the enhancement of decision-making processes. By grounding actions in factual evidence, police officers can make informed decisions that are more likely to lead to positive outcomes. For instance, data-driven hotspot policing, which focuses resources on areas with high crime rates, has been shown to reduce crime more effectively than random patrols.

Enhanced Accountability and Transparency

Evidence-based policing promotes accountability and transparency within law enforcement agencies. By documenting and analyzing the impact of various interventions, agencies can demonstrate their commitment to effective and ethical policing practices. This transparency fosters trust between the police and the communities they serve, as citizens can see that actions are based on objective evidence rather than personal biases.

Reduction in Bias and Discrimination

Relying on factual evidence helps mitigate the influence of implicit biases that can affect intuitive decision-making. Evidence-based approaches prioritize fairness and objectivity, reducing the likelihood of racial profiling and discriminatory practices. For example, randomized control trials in stop-and-search operations have shown that data-driven approaches can significantly decrease racial disparities.

THE DANGERS OF INTUITIVE POLICING

Cognitive Biases in Decision-Making

Intuitive policing is susceptible to a range of cognitive biases that can distort judgment.

Common biases include:

- Confirmation Bias: The tendency to seek out information that confirms pre-existing beliefs while ignoring contradictory evidence.
- Availability Heuristic: Relying on immediate examples that come to mind when evaluating a situation leads to skewed perceptions of reality.
- Anchoring Bias: The influence of initial information on subsequent judgments, even when irrelevant or misleading.

These biases can lead to flawed decision-making, resulting in negative outcomes for both law enforcement officers and the communities they serve.

Erosion of Public Trust

When policing is perceived as arbitrary or biased, public trust erodes. Communities are less likely to cooperate with law enforcement, report crimes, or provide valuable information. This breakdown in trust can create a cycle of increased crime and decreased cooperation, undermining the effectiveness of policing efforts.

CASE STUDIES IN EVIDENCE-BASED POLICING

Operation Ceasefire

One of the most well-known examples of evidence-based policing is Operation Ceasefire, a gun violence reduction strategy implemented in Boston in the mid-1990s. This initiative utilized data analysis to identify key individuals and groups involved in gun violence. By focusing resources on these targets and employing a combination of enforcement and community outreach, Operation Ceasefire achieved a significant reduction in youth homicides.

Problem-Oriented Policing in Newport News

The Newport News Police Department in Virginia successfully applied a problem-oriented policing approach to address burglary issues in a public housing community. By analyzing crime data, officers identified patterns and implemented targeted interventions, such as improving lighting and securing vacant properties. This evidence-based strategy resulted in a 60% reduction in burglaries.

THE INTEGRATION OF TECHNOLOGY IN EVIDENCE-BASED POLICING

Predictive Policing

Predictive policing uses algorithms and data analysis to forecast potential criminal activity. By analyzing historical crime data, social media activity, and environmental factors, predictive models can identify areas and individuals at high risk for criminal behavior. This technology allows law enforcement to allocate resources more effectively and prevent crime before it occurs.

Body-Worn Cameras

The use of body-worn cameras (BWCs) has become increasingly prevalent in evidence-based policing. BWCs provide an objective record of police interactions, promoting accountability and transparency. Research has shown that the presence of BWCs can reduce the use of force incidents and complaints against officers, contributing to improved community relations.

Crime Mapping and Geographic Information Systems (GIS)

Crime mapping and GIS technology enable law enforcement agencies to visualize crime patterns and trends spatially. By analyzing geographic data, police departments can identify hotspots, deploy resources strategically, and develop targeted interventions. This approach enhances the effectiveness of crime prevention efforts and improves resource allocation.

OVERCOMING CHALLENGES IN IMPLEMENTING EVIDENCE-BASED POLICING

Resistance to Change

One of the primary challenges in adopting evidence-based policing is resistance to change within law enforcement agencies. Traditional policing practices and cultural norms can hinder the acceptance of new methodologies. Overcoming this resistance requires strong leadership, effective communication, and a commitment to ongoing training and education.

Data Quality and Availability

The success of evidence-based policing relies heavily on the quality and availability of data. Inaccurate or incomplete data can lead to flawed analyses and misguided interventions. Law enforcement agencies must invest in robust data collection systems and ensure data accuracy to maximize the effectiveness of evidence-based strategies.

Balancing Proactive and Reactive Policing

While evidence-based policing emphasizes proactive strategies, it is essential to balance proactive and reactive approaches. Law enforcement agencies must respond effectively to immediate incidents while implementing long-term, data-driven solutions. Achieving this balance requires careful planning, resource allocation, and collaboration with community stakeholders.

THE FUTURE OF EVIDENCE-BASED POLICING

Increased Collaboration and Partnerships

The future of evidence-based policing lies in increased collaboration and partnerships between law enforcement agencies, academic institutions, and community organizations. By working together, these stakeholders can conduct rigorous research, share best practices, and develop innovative solutions to complex policing challenges.

Advancements in Technology and Analytics

Advancements in technology and data analytics will continue to shape the future of evidence-based policing. Artificial intelligence, machine learning, and big data analytics hold the potential to revolutionize crime prevention and intervention strategies. Law enforcement agencies must stay at the forefront of technological advancements to harness their full potential.

Focus on Community Engagement

As evidence-based policing evolves, there will be an increased focus on community engagement and collaboration. Building trust and legitimacy within communities is essential for effective policing. Law enforcement agencies must actively involve community members in decision-making processes, prioritize transparency, and address community concerns to foster positive relationships.

In the ever-evolving landscape of law enforcement, evidence-based policing emerges as a critical approach that prioritizes facts over intuition. By grounding decisions in empirical evidence, law enforcement agencies can improve decision-making, enhance accountability, and reduce bias. The integration of technology, collaboration, and community engagement further strengthens the effectiveness of evidence-based strategies. As the future of policing unfolds, embracing evidence-based practices will be essential to building trust, fostering safer communities, and ensuring justice for all.

Exploring today's policing strategies, particularly the distinction between facts and assumptions, reveals significant implications for both police officers and those wrongfully convicted due to inaccurate assumptions. This discussion highlights the importance of evidence-based practices in law enforcement, addressing the potential consequences for officers and the impact on individuals subject to wrongful convictions.

Facts vs. Assumptions in Policing Strategies

Modern policing strategies have evolved significantly, emphasizing the importance of relying on factual evidence rather than assumptions. Here's a look at how these strategies operate:

Facts-Based Policing

- Evidence-Based Approaches: This includes strategies that rely on data analysis, crime statistics, and empirical research to inform decision-making. Techniques such as crime mapping, predictive policing, and hotspot analysis fall under this category.

- Community Policing: Engaging with the community to gather information and foster trust, ensuring that actions are based on reliable and firsthand information.

- Use of Technology: Body-worn cameras, surveillance technology, and data analytics tools provide factual evidence to support law enforcement activities.

Assumptions-Based Policing

- Relying on Intuition: Officers may make decisions based on gut feelings or preconceived notions rather than empirical evidence.

- Stereotyping and Bias: Rather than taking into account the most recent evidence, assumptions can lead to biased actions and profiling.

- Reactive Policing: Responding to incidents based on assumptions about the situation or individuals involved rather than gathering comprehensive evidence.

CONSEQUENCES FOR POLICE OFFICERS WHEN THEY ARE NOT CORRECT

When police officers make decisions based on incorrect assumptions, several potential consequences can arise:

Professional Consequences

- Disciplinary Action: Officers may face disciplinary measures, including suspension, demotion, or termination, if their actions based on incorrect assumptions lead to misconduct or violations of policy.

- Legal Accountability: Officers may be subject to civil lawsuits for wrongful actions, resulting in financial penalties and damage to their reputation.

- Loss of Trust: Missteps based on assumptions can erode public trust in law enforcement, leading to strained relationships with the community and reduced cooperation.

Personal Consequences

- Emotional and Psychological Impact: Officers may experience stress, anxiety, and guilt when their actions result in negative outcomes, particularly if they lead to wrongful convictions or harm to individuals.

- Career Impact: Repeated errors based on assumptions can hinder career advancement and opportunities for promotion within the police force.

CONSEQUENCES FOR THE WRONGFULLY CONVICTED

When individuals are wrongfully convicted due to policing based on incorrect assumptions, the impacts can be severe and long-lasting:

Legal Consequences

- Incarceration: Wrongful convictions often lead to unjust imprisonment, depriving individuals of their freedom and subjecting them to the challenges of life in prison.

- Criminal Record: A wrongful conviction leaves individuals with a criminal record, which can have lasting impacts on their ability to find employment, housing, and education.

Personal and Social Consequences

- Emotional and Psychological Trauma: The experience of being wrongfully convicted can cause significant emotional distress, including anxiety, depression, and post-traumatic stress disorder (PTSD).

- Stigma and Isolation: Those who are wrongfully convicted may face social stigma and isolation, impacting their relationships with family and friends.

Economic Consequences

- Financial Hardship: The costs associated with legal defense, lost employment opportunities, and the potential for ongoing legal battles can lead to significant financial hardship for wrongfully convicted individuals and their families.

ADDRESSING AND MITIGATING THE CONSEQUENCES

For Police Officers

- Training and Education: Providing officers with ongoing training on evidence-based practices, implicit bias, and cultural competency can reduce reliance on assumptions and improve decision-making.

- Accountability Measures: Implementing robust accountability systems, including oversight bodies and transparent investigations, can ensure officers are held accountable for their actions.

- Support and Resources: Offering support services, such as counseling and peer support programs, can help officers cope with the emotional and psychological impact of their work.

CHAPTER 04

HISTORICAL MOVEMENTS AND INCENTIVES IN POLICING (1960s–2000s)

Since the 1960s, the landscape of policing in the United States has undergone significant changes driven by social movements, legislative changes, and shifting community expectations. The role of police unions, significant legislative acts, and technological advancements have all played pivotal roles in shaping modern policing practices, and understanding these historical contexts is crucial for comprehending current debates and ongoing efforts to reform and improve law enforcement.

Policing is a physically and emotionally demanding profession. The stress associated with law enforcement duties, including the risk of physical harm, exposure to traumatic events, and the high-stakes nature of decision-making, can contribute to burnout and the need for earlier retirement compared to less demanding careers.

During the 1960s and 1970s, the incentives for becoming a police officer were relatively modest, with a primary focus on salary, job stability, and pensions. Police officers earned an average annual salary ranging from $5,000 to $8,000, offering modest compensation by today's standards but stable employment in an era marked by economic volatility. Defined benefit pensions were also a significant incentive, providing officers with a steady income after retirement based on years of service and final salary—a major draw for those seeking financial security. Social prestige was another appealing aspect of policing, as it was considered a respected profession imbued with a sense of duty and pride in government service. However, the Civil Rights Movement, coupled with extensive media coverage of police brutality, exposed substantial racial discrimination and abuses within law enforcement. This led to growing distrust and criticism of the police, particularly among minority communities, with high-profile incidents and the aggressive tactics of the War on Drugs further straining public perception and intensifying debates over law enforcement practices and individual rights.

By the 1980s through the 2000s, incentives for police officers evolved and expanded, reflecting broader efforts toward the professionalization of the field. New and enhanced incentives were introduced to attract a diverse pool of candidates and to address the complex demands of modern policing. In the 1980s through the 2000s, incentives for joining the police force evolved significantly, reflecting broader changes in societal expectations and the professionalization of law enforcement.

The War on Drugs, initiated by President Nixon and escalated under the Reagan administration, significantly shaped policing by increasing funding for police departments and enhancing resources available to officers. This era introduced a shift towards more aggressive policing tactics, aimed at curbing drug-related crimes but often leading to heightened tensions within communities. Alongside these changes, community policing emerged as a strategy focused on building relationships between officers and community members to address local issues collaboratively, fostering greater engagement and trust. During this period, police unions also gained strength and influence, securing better pay, benefits, and improved working conditions for officers.

These unions played a pivotal role in negotiating competitive salaries and comprehensive pension plans that elevated the financial appeal of policing as a career.

Legislative acts during this period also had profound impacts on policing practices and officer incentives. In the 1960s and 1970s, groundbreaking reforms transformed police procedures, such as the 1966 Supreme Court decision in *Miranda v. Arizona*, which mandated that officers inform suspects of their rights. This ruling fundamentally altered police interactions with suspects and set new standards for procedural fairness. Additionally, the Civil Rights Movement underscored widespread concerns about police brutality and racial discrimination, catalyzing demands for reform and greater accountability in law enforcement. In the following decades, legislation continued to reshape policing. The 1994 Violent Crime Control and Law Enforcement Act, often called Clinton's Crime Bill, funded the hiring of 100,000 new officers, expanded the death penalty, and enacted the "three strikes" rule, contributing to significant increases in incarceration rates. Following the 9/11 attacks, new federal legislation expanded law enforcement powers, leading to the creation of the Department of Homeland Security and increased federal oversight and resources for local policing. These legislative changes emphasized a more security-focused approach to law enforcement, reflecting evolving national priorities.

From the 1960s to today, policing has seen substantial changes, especially in terms of salaries and pension structures. In the 1960s and 1970s, police officer salaries were relatively modest, with job security often outweighing financial incentives. Compensation was not high, yet the stability of a government job was appealing to many. By contrast, from the 2000s onward, salaries have increased significantly.

Pension structures have also evolved. In the earlier decades, defined benefit pensions were standard, guaranteeing officers a set retirement income based on years of service and final salary. This reliable retirement income was a core incentive. While many departments still offer defined benefit pensions, there has been a gradual shift towards defined contribution plans in some areas due to budget constraints. Nonetheless, police departments generally continue to provide competitive pension packages, which remain a major attraction for those entering the profession.

Today, incentives for joining the police force have become more comprehensive, reflecting the evolving needs and expectations of the profession. Law enforcement today offers numerous incentives that make it a financially and professionally attractive career. Competitive salaries, supplemented by overtime pay and bonuses, enhance its appeal, providing substantial earning potential. Comprehensive benefits packages, including health insurance, life insurance, and paid time off—often extending to officers' families—add to the profession's allure. Robust pension plans ensure financial security in retirement, while the stability of law enforcement careers offers a low risk of layoffs, providing job security. Additionally, there are extensive opportunities for career advancement and specialization, such as roles in SWAT, K-9 units, and cybercrime, which foster growth and professional development. For many, the desire to serve and protect their communities is a powerful motivator, reinforcing the sense of purpose in this field. Modern policing also involves the use of advanced technology, appealing to those interested in tech-driven careers. Furthermore, strong police unions play a significant role in negotiating better salaries, working conditions, and legal protections, collectively enhancing the attractiveness of the profession. 5. Regional Variations in the United States

The incentives and conditions for policing vary widely between different regions within the United States, influenced by factors such as cost of living, state budgets, and union strength. Law enforcement incentives vary significantly across the United States, with notable differences by region. On the East Coast, New York City's NYPD offers high starting salaries and robust pension plans, supported by powerful unions. The elevated cost of living in New York City justifies these higher salaries. Massachusetts also provides competitive salaries and strong pensions, bolstered by influential police unions, making law enforcement positions attractive in the state.

On the West Coast, California offers some of the highest police salaries nationwide, alongside generous pension plans and powerful unions. Cities like Los Angeles and San Francisco provide competitive starting salaries and comprehensive benefits packages. Oregon and Washington also offer competitive pay with defined benefit pension plans and influential unions that support officers' needs and rights.

In the Southern states, Texas exhibits considerable variation in police salaries, with higher pay and strong union presence in major cities. Defined benefit pension plans are common throughout the state, providing financial security for officers. Florida offers higher salaries in larger cities, coupled with defined benefit plans and active unions that work to improve conditions for officers. In contrast, North Carolina generally has lower police salaries and less influential unions, though defined benefit pension plans remain a part of the compensation structure.6. Variations Between Countries: United States vs. United Kingdom

Police salaries, pension plans, union influence, and public perception of law enforcement vary significantly between the United States and the United Kingdom. In terms of salaries, U.S. police officers generally earn higher wages, with considerable variation depending on the state and city. In contrast, UK police salaries are typically lower, with starting salaries for constables ranging from £24,000 to £30,000 (equivalent to $30,000–$38,000). Pension plans also differ; many U.S. departments offer defined benefit pensions, although some regions are moving toward defined contribution plans. In the UK, the Police Pension Scheme provides defined benefit pensions, although recent reforms have adjusted contribution rates and benefits.

Union influence is notably stronger in the United States, where police unions play a significant role in negotiating pay, benefits, and protections for officers. In the UK, the Police Federation acts as a representative body and offers a level of collective bargaining, but its influence is generally more limited than that of U.S. police unions. Community policing and public perception also vary. In the United States, approaches to community policing differ widely, with some areas emphasizing relationship-building while others struggle with public trust, especially in light of high-profile incidents involving police misconduct. In the United Kingdom, community policing is a central focus, aiming to foster strong relationships between officers and the public. While public perception of UK police is generally more positive, there are ongoing challenges and criticisms similar to those faced in the U.S.

Technology, equipment, training, and professional development in policing differ between the United States and the United Kingdom. In the U.S., law enforcement agencies have extensive access to advanced technology, including body cameras, drones, and sophisticated forensic tools. Many departments can also acquire military-grade equipment through programs like the 1033 program, which enhances their capabilities in various situations. Conversely, the United Kingdom also employs advanced technology, but with stricter restrictions on military-grade equipment. UK policing emphasizes less-lethal options and de-escalation techniques, aligning with a focus on minimizing force.

In terms of training and professional development, the U.S. has varying standards across states and departments, with larger departments typically offering more comprehensive training and development opportunities. In contrast, the United Kingdom has national standards for police training, ensuring consistency and emphasizing continuous professional development. The College of Policing sets these standards and provides training programs, creating a more unified approach to professional development across the country.

There are significant differences in policing incentives, practices, and conditions across the East Coast, West Coast, and Southern states in the United States. Living expenses, state budgets, union strength, and regional political and social climates are just a few examples of the variables that affect these differences.

Since the 1960s, policing has evolved considerably due to social movements, legislation, and changing societal needs. Comparing policing in the 1970s to the present reveals significant shifts in incentives, legislative impacts, and the influence of historical events on law enforcement. In the 1960s and 1970s, incentives for entering the police force were relatively straightforward, with a primary focus on modest salaries, job stability, and pensions. The role was highly regarded, and the promise of stable government employment made it attractive. Police unions existed during this period, but they were limited in influence, primarily focusing on securing job stability, reasonable working conditions, and advocating for fair salary negotiations.

In the 2000s and beyond, incentives in policing have expanded, with officers now receiving higher salaries, enhanced benefits, and generous pension plans. Technological advancements have led to specialized roles within law enforcement, which often come with additional responsibilities and higher pay. Police unions today hold much greater power, playing a crucial role in advocating for policies that protect officers' rights, such as qualified immunity.

They are instrumental in negotiating better salaries and benefits for officers and have become prominent voices in resisting certain reforms, especially in cases involving officer misconduct. This shift highlights the growing complexity of policing and the increased focus on supporting law enforcement professionals in an ever-evolving landscape.

Regional differences across the U.S. significantly influence law enforcement careers, affecting the appeal, challenges, and opportunities available to officers.

On the East Coast, cities like New York and Philadelphia experience high levels of crime and violence, especially in densely populated urban areas. These conditions create more opportunities for officers to pursue specialized training and career advancement in areas like anti-terrorism, cybercrime, and community policing. For many, these paths are attractive, offering a chance to make a substantial impact and gain valuable experience. However, the high-stress nature of these environments, coupled with the potential dangers officers face, can be deterrents for some. The decision to pursue a law enforcement career on the East Coast often balances the desire for impactful work, the availability of specialized roles, and the strong support provided by influential police unions.

On the West Coast, cities such as Los Angeles and San Francisco confront unique issues like gang violence and homelessness, which shape the law enforcement landscape. These challenges lead to opportunities for officers to specialize in gang prevention, mental health crisis intervention, and community engagement. The progressive political climate on the West Coast also encourages initiatives for police reform and innovative practices, drawing individuals who are interested in modernizing law enforcement. Although the cost of living is high in many West Coast cities, competitive salaries and comprehensive benefits make the profession appealing. For many aspiring officers, the decision to work in West Coast law enforcement stems from a blend of financial motivation, career growth opportunities, and a commitment to addressing complex social issues.

In the southern states, the appeal of a law enforcement career is influenced by regional crime levels and economic conditions. Areas with lower crime rates may offer fewer opportunities for specialized training and advancement, but they often provide a more stable and less stressful working environment. Conversely, cities with higher crime rates, such as New Orleans and Memphis, present opportunities for officers to gain experience in high-pressure situations and advance to specialized units. The cost of living in

Southern states is generally lower, making the financial incentives more appealing despite lower average salaries compared to the East and West Coasts.

The cultural emphasis on community and traditional values can enhance the appeal of law enforcement careers in these regions. The decision to pursue a career in law enforcement in the South is multifaceted, influenced by the balance between financial incentives, career opportunities, and the desire to serve in a community-oriented environment.

From the 1960s to the present, the landscape of policing has undergone significant changes due to social movements, legislation, and evolving societal needs. Salaries, pensions, and other incentives have improved, making law enforcement a more attractive career. However, significant variations exist between different regions within the United States and internationally, influenced by the cost of living, union strength, and local political climates. Despite these differences, policing remains an enticing career due to the combination of financial rewards, job stability, and the opportunity to serve the community.

CHAPTER 05

MILITARY EXPERIENCE AND POLICING

Thishis chapter explores the parallels between military experience and policing, highlighting how the skills and training acquired in one field can be applied to the other. The transition from military service to civilian life presents numerous challenges, particularly in securing employment. However, the skills and experiences acquired in the military are highly valued in many civilian professions, particularly in law enforcement. According to a report by Walker (2010), veterans and non-veterans aged between 18 and 54 are employed at the same rate, underscoring the adaptability and relevance of military skills in the civilian workforce.

Military experience equips veterans with essential skills directly applicable to policing, making them well-suited for careers in law enforcement. By examining the transferable skills and qualities gained through military service, such as leadership, teamwork, and problem-solving abilities, this chapter aims to provide insights into how veterans can successfully transition into law enforcement roles. It will address the unique challenges that veterans may face during the transition process and offer strategies for overcoming them.

Military experience instills in veterans a strong sense of discipline and commitment, highly valued traits in law enforcement. Additionally, the structured environment of the military helps veterans adapt to the similarly structured nature of police work, enhancing their effectiveness in this new career path.

However, while the parallels between military service and policing offer numerous advantages, this transition is not without its challenges. Veterans may encounter difficulties in adjusting to the different dynamics of civilian law enforcement, such as the emphasis on community-oriented policing versus the more hierarchical and command-driven nature of military operations. Moreover, the high stress environments experienced in both the military and policing can have cumulative effects on mental health, requiring careful consideration and support during the transition.

This chapter will weigh the pros and cons of utilizing military experience in policing, exploring how the strengths of military training can be harnessed while also addressing the potential pitfalls and stresses that veterans might encounter in their law enforcement careers. By providing a balanced perspective, this chapter aims to equip veterans, law enforcement agencies, and policymakers with the knowledge needed to facilitate a successful and sustainable transition from military service to policing.

Veterans might encounter in their law enforcement careers, ultimately leading to a more effective and supportive environment for those making the transition.

THE VALUE OF MILITARY SKILLS IN CIVILIAN EMPLOYMENT

Military service instills a wide range of skills that are highly transferable to civilian careers. These include, but are not limited to, discipline, leadership, teamwork, and the ability to work under pressure. Veterans bring a strong work ethic, a sense of duty, and a commitment to service—qualities that are invaluable in any workplace. Walker (2010) notes that these attributes contribute to the comparable employment rates between veterans and non-veterans in the 18-54 age group, indicating that employers recognize and appreciate the unique capabilities that veterans bring to the table.

Pros:

- Discipline and Structure: Veterans are accustomed to operating within a structured environment, which translates well to the civilian workforce. This discipline is particularly beneficial in roles that require adherence to protocols, such as in law enforcement or corporate settings.

- Leadership and Teamwork: Military training emphasizes leadership and the importance of working as part of a cohesive team. These skills are directly applicable to many civilian careers, especially in roles where collaboration and leadership are essential.

- Problem-Solving and Adaptability: Veterans often possess strong problem-solving abilities and adaptability, making them valuable assets in dynamic work environments. Their experience in diverse and challenging situations equips them with the resilience and determination needed to excel in various roles.

- Work Ethic and Commitment: Military experience fosters a strong work ethic and a commitment to completing tasks to the best of one's ability. Employers benefit from hiring veterans who bring this level of dedication and perseverance to their roles.

Cons:

- Transition Challenges: Despite their valuable skills, veterans may struggle with adapting to a different work culture or finding a sense of purpose outside of the military. The civilian workplace may lack the camaraderie and structure veterans are accustomed to, leading to feelings of isolation or frustration.

- Overqualification: In some cases, veterans may be perceived as overqualified for certain positions, leading to challenges in securing employment that matches their skill level and experience.

- Mental Health Considerations: The stresses of military service, especially for those who have seen combat, can lead to mental health challenges such as PTSD, which may impact their ability to function effectively in a civilian job without proper support.

- Perception Issues: Some employers may have misconceptions about veterans, such as assuming they might struggle with authority or have difficulty adjusting to non-military environments. These perceptions can create barriers to employment for veterans.

COMMUNICATION AND INTERPERSONAL SKILLS

One of the most critical skills acquired during military service is communication. In the military, effective communication is not only about conveying information clearly and concisely but also about understanding and interpreting orders, often in high-stress environments. These skills translate seamlessly into law enforcement, where clear communication is essential for both officer safety and public interaction.

Pros:

- Effective Communication: Military veterans are adept at building strong relationships and fostering teamwork, which are crucial in law enforcement settings. Their ability to effectively communicate with diverse groups of people allows them to de-escalate tense situations and build trust within communities.

- Crisis Management: Veterans are trained to think quickly on their feet and adapt to rapidly changing situations, making them valuable assets in law enforcement roles. Their experience in following strict protocols and procedures also aligns well with the structured nature of police work.

- Team Cohesion: The military places a strong emphasis on teamwork and cooperation, often requiring individuals from diverse backgrounds to work together to achieve common goals. In policing, these interpersonal skills are crucial for building community relationships, de-escalating tense situations, and working collaboratively with fellow officers.

- Cultural Competence: Veterans' experience in working with people from different backgrounds and cultures can be a valuable asset in de-escalating conflicts and building positive relationships within the community.

Cons:

- Communication Style: The direct and authoritative communication style often used in the military may not always be well-received in civilian or law enforcement settings, where a more nuanced approach might be required.

- Adapting to New Protocols: While veterans are skilled in following military protocols, they may need time and training to adjust to the different procedures and expectations in civilian law enforcement, which might prioritize community policing and relationship-building.

- Mental Health Stigma: Veterans may face stigma related to mental health issues, which can impact their communication and interpersonal interactions in the workplace. This can lead to misunderstandings or difficulty in fully integrating into a new team.

- Transition from Combat Mindset: Veterans accustomed to high-pressure, combat-oriented environments may need to adjust their communication and interpersonal approaches when transitioning to the often more community-focused and less adversarial field of law enforcement.

- These sections provide a balanced view of the pros and cons associated with military skills and how they translate into civilian employment and law enforcement roles. The analysis highlights both the strengths and potential challenges veterans may face as they transition into new careers.

VERBAL AND WRITTEN SKILLS

Military training also places a significant emphasis on verbal and written communication. Veterans are trained to give and receive orders clearly, often in fast-paced and stressful situations. This ability to articulate thoughts and instructions effectively is invaluable in law enforcement, where officers must often give clear commands, provide detailed reports, and communicate with various stakeholders, including the public, legal professionals, and fellow officers.

Veterans are typically accustomed to working in high-pressure environments and making split-second decisions, skills that are crucial in law enforcement. Their experience in handling intense situations and remaining calm under pressure can be a valuable asset when dealing with emergencies and dangerous situations on the job. Military training sets the foundation for many of the skills necessary for a successful career in law enforcement, such as discipline, teamwork, and problem-solving abilities.

Veterans often bring a strong sense of duty and commitment to serving and protecting their communities, making them well-suited for the demands of a career in law enforcement. Having a hand up on these skills can give veterans a competitive edge in the field and make them valuable assets to any law enforcement agency. Their ability to adapt to different environments and work well under stress can help them excel in the dynamic and unpredictable nature of police work.

There could be a downfall to the veterans who only did combat and didn't receive training in filing written reports, community policing, or de-escalation techniques, but with the right support and resources, they can still be successful in law enforcement. Agencies that prioritize ongoing training and professional development for their veteran hires can help them bridge any gaps in their skill set and ensure they continue to thrive in their new career.

Written skills, in particular, are crucial in policing. Law enforcement officers are required to document incidents thoroughly and accurately, often under tight deadlines. Veterans, accustomed to maintaining detailed records and reports in the military, are normally well prepared for this aspect of policing. Veterans are often trained in conflict resolution and de-escalation techniques, which can be extremely beneficial when dealing with potentially volatile situations in law enforcement. The downfall of the few who did not have the necessary training to properly fill out written reports highlights the importance of strong written communication skills in law enforcement, especially when accuracy and detail are crucial for legal proceedings. Training is received, of course; however, continued practice and ongoing education are essential for maintaining and improving these skills over time.

On the other hand, most veterans bring a unique set of experiences and training that can greatly benefit police departments in maintaining accurate documentation and effectively resolving conflicts. Their ability to think quickly on their feet and adapt to changing circumstances can also be a valuable asset in the field. Not everyone is equipped to write detailed reports quickly and effectively, making veterans a valuable asset in law enforcement agencies. Their experience in high-pressure situations and commitment to following procedures can help ensure that incidents are properly documented and resolved.

LEADERSHIP AND DECISION-MAKING

Leadership is another area where veterans often excel. Leadership is an area that is not often taught in traditional educational settings, but veterans have gained valuable experience in this area through their military service. Leaders are born every day, but they excel at making tough decisions under pressure and guiding their teams towards success. Veterans bring a unique perspective to leadership roles, drawing on their training and experience to inspire and motivate those around them.

Depending on the area of leadership, veterans may also have specialized skills such as crisis management, strategic planning, and conflict resolution. Their ability to adapt to changing situations and remain calm under stress can be invaluable in a variety of leadership positions. What makes one a leader is not just their title or position, but their ability to inspire and influence others towards a common goal. Veterans often possess the qualities of courage, integrity, and selflessness that are essential for effective leadership in any setting. These qualities, combined with their experience and skills, make veterans valuable assets in leadership roles across various industries. Men and women who have served in the military bring a unique perspective and set of skills to the table that can greatly benefit policing. Their dedication to teamwork and mission accomplishment is unmatched, making them ideal candidates for leadership positions in both the public and private sectors.

Military service frequently places individuals in positions of responsibility, requiring them to make quick decisions, often with limited information and under significant pressure. These leadership experiences prepare veterans for the challenges of policing, where officers must often take charge of situations, make split-second decisions, and lead by example. In leadership, veterans can draw on their experiences in the military to effectively manage teams, communicate clearly, and prioritize tasks in high-stress environments. Their ability to remain calm under pressure and inspire confidence in others can make them strong leaders within a police force.

A leader knows where to focus their attention and resources to achieve the desired outcomes, and veterans have the strategic mindset and adaptability to excel in this aspect. Their commitment to serving and protecting their community aligns with the core values of law enforcement, making them natural leaders in a police force. A natural leader will also possess strong problem-solving skills and the ability to think quickly on their feet, both of which are essential in law enforcement situations where split-second decisions can have significant consequences. These men and women often have experience working collaboratively with diverse teams, which is crucial in a police force that requires cooperation and unity among its members to effectively serve and protect the community.

The decision-making skills developed in the military are particularly relevant in law enforcement, where officers must assess situations rapidly, weigh the potential consequences of their actions, and make choices that prioritize public safety and uphold the law. Veterans' ability to remain calm under pressure and make sound decisions is a significant asset in these scenarios.

Thinking quickly on your feet is essential in high-stress situations that law enforcement officers often encounter. The discipline and dedication instilled in military veterans can translate seamlessly into the demanding and unpredictable nature of police work. There are times when a person doesn't have time to call a situation in but must act immediately to prevent harm or diffuse a dangerous situation. Veterans' training and experience in making split-second decisions can be invaluable in these critical moments, potentially saving lives and maintaining order.

Decision making skills homed in the military can also be crucial in navigating complex legal and ethical dilemmas that law enforcement officers face on a daily basis. Where one officer might struggle to weigh the risks and benefits of a particular course of action, a veteran may be able to draw on their past experiences to make a more informed decision. Veterans often bring a strong sense of duty and commitment to serving and protecting their communities, qualities that are essential in law enforcement. This is not to limit what another person without the military background can bring to the table, but rather to highlight the unique perspective and skills that veterans can offer in this field. The discipline and resilience instilled in veterans through their military training can help them effectively handle high-pressure situations and remain calm under stress, making them valuable assets in law enforcement roles.

THE TRANSITION TO LAW ENFORCEMENT

For many veterans, law enforcement offers a natural transition from military service. The transition is often seamless due to the similarities in structure, hierarchy, and mission-driven focus between the military and law enforcement. The sense of duty and commitment to serving and protecting others that veterans possess aligns well with the responsibilities of a law enforcement officer. When one is preparing to exit the military, pursuing a career in law enforcement can provide a sense of continuity and purpose. The skills and experiences gained during military service can be directly applicable to the demands of a law enforcement role. Both fields require a commitment to serving and protecting others, and both demand a high level of discipline, integrity, and courage.

The structure and camaraderie of a police force can also provide a sense of familiarity and belonging for veterans, easing the transition into civilian life. Furthermore, many law enforcement agencies actively seek out veterans for recruitment, recognizing the value of their military experience. Programs designed to support veterans in their transition to civilian careers often include pathways into law enforcement, providing training and resources to help veterans adapt their military skills to the specific demands of policing.

Military experience provides veterans with a strong foundation of skills that are highly applicable to careers in law enforcement. The communication, interpersonal, verbal, and written skills developed in the military are directly relevant to the demands of policing, making veterans well-suited for this line of work. As Walker (2010) suggests, the comparable employment rates between veterans and non-veterans in the civilian workforce highlight the value of military skills in various professions, particularly in law enforcement. By leveraging their military experience, veterans can continue to serve their communities with honor and distinction, finding fulfillment in a career that aligns with their skills and values.

Military experience and policing have their benefits, as veterans bring a unique perspective and level of discipline to the job that can enhance overall effectiveness in maintaining public safety. The structured training and leadership experience gained in the military can also contribute to successful outcomes in law enforcement roles. Men and women who have served in the armed forces bring a valuable skill set to the field that can include crisis management, teamwork, and a strong work ethic. Their ability to remain calm under pressure and adapt to challenging situations can be invaluable in law enforcement roles. Their experiences in the military can make them well-suited for a variety of law enforcement positions.

By joining the police force, military members can continue to serve their communities and uphold the values they fought for while also transitioning into a new career path that aligns with their skills and experiences. Their understanding of discipline, respect for authority, and commitment to duty make them well-respected members of law enforcement agencies. Strength and duty are key attributes that military members bring to the police force, allowing them to effectively protect and serve their communities. Their ability to work well in teams and follow strict protocols further enhances their effectiveness in law enforcement roles.

CHAPTER 06

THE EXAMINATION OF VIABLE RESEARCH BETWEEN TURKISH AND US POLICE OFFICERS

The examination of viable research on police officers' education levels and performance reveals a strong correlation between higher education and improved job performance. Studies, such as those by Leedy and Ormrod (2005) and Beyhan (2008), indicate that education enhances officers' ability to handle complex tasks, navigate legal procedures, and engage with their communities. The use of correlational research designs, as outlined by Leedy and Ormrod, enables researchers to identify relationships between key variables like education and performance. This method is well-suited for examining police officers because it allows the collection of data across multiple characteristics, such as job preparedness, performance reviews, and disciplinary records, providing a comprehensive understanding of how education impacts their careers.

Research by Beyhan (2008) on Turkish police officers found similar results, demonstrating that officers with a college education were better prepared for the challenges of modern policing. This aligns with findings in the U.S., where officers with bachelor's degrees or higher tend to perform better and receive more commendations, promotions, and positive citizen reviews. However, the research highlights limitations in relying on self-reported surveys, which can inflate performance metrics. While Beyhan's study acknowledged these limitations, the longitudinal research conducted by Truxillo et al. (1998) provided a more objective analysis, measuring officers' promotions and disciplinary actions over a 10-year period. This approach confirmed that officers with higher education levels had fewer disciplinary issues and better career outcomes.

The examination of viable research underscores the importance of considering longitudinal designs to measure performance over time. Truxillo et al. (1998) noted that while cross-sectional surveys can provide useful snapshots, they fail to capture the progression of officers' careers, such as the impact of continuing education after being hired. Longitudinal studies enable a deeper understanding of how education acquired during an officer's tenure influences long-term performance, promotions, and professional development. This comprehensive approach provides valuable insights into the long-term benefits of higher education in law enforcement and supports the case for promoting educational advancement within police departments.

A 10-year plan in law enforcement offers officers and departments a framework for career development, educational growth, and performance evaluations. With education playing an increasingly significant role in law enforcement, understanding the impact of various levels of college education on job performance is essential. A 10-year plan in the context of law enforcement provides a strategic framework for officers' career development, performance evaluations, and educational growth. Police departments often rely on longitudinal research to assess the impact of factors like education, experience, and promotions on an officer's overall effectiveness. However, there are still many challenges in accurately measuring and analyzing these factors.

In law enforcement, long-term planning is essential for career growth and departmental success. A 10-year plan allows officers and departments to set specific goals related to performance, promotions, and educational advancements. Having a structured timeline encourages officers to stay on track, providing measurable benchmarks for their growth and skill development. According to Truxillo, Bennett, and Collins (1998), one of the key reasons for conducting a longitudinal investigation is that it enables researchers to track the officers' progression during a fixed period—typically 10 years—which includes promotions and disciplinary actions received. By setting clear long-term goals, officers can be evaluated more effectively, leading to better decision-making regarding promotions and assignments. This long-term perspective is also crucial for departments looking to have a more stable and professional workforce. By implementing a 10-year plan, officers are motivated to focus on continual professional development, ensuring that they remain engaged and committed to their role.

On average, police officers serve between 20 and 30 years, depending on their department and career aspirations. Many officers achieve major career milestones, such as promotions or specialized training, within the first 10 years. The early stages of an officer's career, typically within the first 10 years, are often the most formative in terms of performance evaluations, disciplinary actions, and promotions. Truxillo et al. (1998) observed that the initial 10-year span of an officer's career can provide valuable insights into their ability to adapt, improve, and succeed within the department. This period also often serves as a critical time for educational advancement. Many officers enter the force with a high school diploma or associate degree, but ongoing educational opportunities, such as higher degrees or certifications, frequently arise during the first decade of their career. Leedy and Ormrod (2005) specified that long-term research, such as a 10-year plan, is appropriate for assessing how such education impacts performance. The 10-year timeline gives officers the opportunity to pursue additional education while also meeting their day-to-day responsibilities, thereby creating a more well-rounded law enforcement professional.

The correlation between Turkish officers and U.S. officers concerning education and performance is worth mentioning. Beyhan (2008) found that in both countries, officers with higher education levels generally exhibited better job performance, were promoted more quickly, and received fewer disciplinary actions compared to their peers with less education. Both Turkish and U.S. officers who held bachelor's degrees or higher were more likely to receive commendations, indicating that education has a universal impact on an officer's capacity to perform effectively regardless of the country. This aligns with Leedy and Ormrod's (2005) assertion that correlational research can help identify the relationships between specific characteristics—in this case, education and performance. In both studies, the correlation between higher education levels and better job performance was strong, with officers in both countries receiving more awards and promotions due to their academic achievements. The countries might not have similarities in terms of culture or political systems, but the positive impact of education on job performance seems to be a universal trend among law enforcement officers. This suggests that investing in higher education for officers could lead to improved performance and recognition across different countries. When other countries observe the case studies done between Turkey and the US, they may consider implementing similar educational initiatives for their own law enforcement officers to enhance their job performance and career advancement opportunities. This could ultimately contribute to a more effective and professional law enforcement workforce on a global scale. It is likely that this trend will continue to grow as more countries recognize the benefits of providing higher education opportunities for their law enforcement officers. By investing in education, countries can ensure that their officers are well-equipped to handle the complexities of modern policing and maintain public trust and safety.

Empathy also plays a crucial role in improving relationships between law enforcement officers and the communities they serve. Research has shown that officers who demonstrate empathy towards community members are more likely to de-escalate tense situations and build rapport, leading to increased trust and cooperation. Overall, investing in higher education and developing empathy among law enforcement officers can have a positive impact on community policing efforts. The community will feel safer and more supported by law enforcement. They know the officers who actually care and the ones who are merely doing a job; empathy shows that officers are truly committed to serving and protecting the community, ultimately improving overall public safety. Promoting empathy can help reduce instances of excessive force and misconduct, creating a more positive and collaborative relationship between law enforcement and the community. When an officer is based on empathy, they are better equipped to de-escalate tense situations and build trust with community members, leading to more effective crime prevention and resolution. This shift towards empathy-driven policing can also help address systemic issues and biases within law enforcement, making it a more equitable and just system for all individuals involved. Empathy for the Turkish officers as well as those in the US is crucial in improving understanding and promoting a culture of respect and accountability within law enforcement. By prioritizing empathy in policing practices, officers can work towards creating safer and more inclusive communities for everyone.

Education is a critical factor in determining how well officers are prepared for the complexities of modern policing. Officers with at least a minimum number of college credits typically demonstrate better job preparedness compared to those with only a high school diploma. According to Beyhan (2008), Turkish police officers with college education, especially those with at least some credits in higher education, were better equipped to handle tasks related to critical thinking, problem-solving, and community engagement. U.S. officers with a minimum number of college credits showed higher job preparedness, especially in roles requiring analytical thinking and communication skills. The need for more officers to be educated lies in the increasing complexity of modern policing tasks, which require a higher level of cognitive skills and adaptability. College-educated officers are more likely to understand and effectively address the diverse needs of the communities they serve. This is the urgent need when it comes to improving police-community relations and ensuring equitable and effective law enforcement practices. Higher education can also help officers understand and deal with ethical dilemmas and make informed decisions in high-pressure situations, ultimately leading to better outcomes for both officers and the communities they serve. When there are officers who have less education, they may struggle to effectively communicate and connect with community members, leading to misunderstandings and potential conflicts. Investing in higher education for law enforcement officers can ultimately lead to improved trust, communication, and outcomes within communities.

For officers with a bachelor's degree, studies have shown a more significant impact on job performance and preparedness. Beyhan (2008) emphasized that officers with a bachelor's degree were more likely to demonstrate a deeper understanding of legal procedures, community relations, and conflict resolution. Truxillo et al. (1998) found that these officers also received more positive performance reviews from their superiors, often resulting in promotions and commendations. A bachelor's degree can improve job performance and advancement opportunities for police officers; it ultimately benefits the entire community by ensuring that law enforcement professionals are better equipped to handle complex situations and build positive relationships with residents. Higher education can also lead to increased job satisfaction and overall well-being for officers, contributing to a more effective and responsive police force.

Looking over the results in the surveys taken by police officers who have pursued higher education, the majority report feeling more confident in their abilities to serve and protect the community. This demonstrates the positive impact that further education can have on law enforcement professionals and their effectiveness in carrying out their duties. This goes beyond the call of duty on the street but also at home for the officers, as they are better equipped to handle the mental and emotional challenges that come with the job. This results in a more well-rounded officer who is better able to serve and protect their community and deal with the day-to-day challenges in their personal lives where their families, friends, and neighbors also feel safe and supported.

Officers who surpass the bachelor's degree level, earning graduate-level credits or advanced degrees, demonstrate the highest levels of job preparedness. According to the report, the highest level of education found among officers in the study was a master's degree. These officers tended to occupy leadership roles within their departments and were frequently sought out for specialized training and high-level decision-making roles. Their preparedness was notably higher, as they could better navigate complex legal situations and manage crisis scenarios. When one continues with their education, reaching the master's degree level, they not only enhance their knowledge and skills but also increase their opportunities for career advancement and professional growth. This level of education equips individuals with the expertise needed to excel in leadership positions and make significant contributions to their field. It allows officers to stay current with best practices, industry trends, and cutting-edge research, ultimately making them more effective in their roles. The officers are also aware that the master's degree level can open doors to higher-paying positions and provide a competitive edge in the job market, making them more marketable and sought after by employers.

Pursuing a master's degree can lead to expanded networking opportunities and connections within the industry, further boosting career prospects and potential for success. While one has different reasons for obtaining their master's degree, such as personal growth or career advancement, the overall benefit of increased knowledge and skills cannot be understated. The dedication and commitment required to complete a master's degree program can demonstrate to employers a strong work ethic and determination, further enhancing one's professional reputation. Going the distance to earn a master's degree shows a willingness to invest in oneself and strive for excellence, qualities that are highly valued in today's competitive job market. The advanced education and specialized training gained through a master's program can provide individuals with a competitive edge and set them apart from other candidates who are also interested in the same positions. It's not always a cakewalk, but it's definitely worth the effort in the long run.

The critical thinking skills and expertise acquired can be what ultimately leads to career advancement and increased earning potential. Overall, obtaining a master's degree can open up new opportunities and pave the way for a successful and fulfilling career, as well as having a sense of personal fulfillment and accomplishment.

The correlation between Turkish officers and U.S. officers concerning education and performance is noteworthy. Beyhan (2008) found that in both countries, officers with higher education levels generally exhibited better job performance, were promoted more quickly, and received fewer disciplinary actions compared to their peers with less education. Both Turkish and U.S. officers who held bachelor's degrees or higher were more likely to receive commendations, indicating that education has a universal impact on an officer's capacity to perform effectively regardless of the country. This aligns with Leedy and Ormrod's (2005) assertion that correlational research can help identify the relationships between specific characteristics—in this case, education and performance. In both studies, the correlation between higher education levels and better job performance was strong, with officers in both countries receiving more awards and promotions due to their academic achievements.

Officers with higher education levels tend to receive more awards, promotions, and commendations throughout their careers. Truxillo et al. (1998) noted that U.S. officers with bachelor's degrees or higher were more likely to receive performance-related awards and commendations from both their departments and the public. Additionally, officers with more college credits were promoted faster and more frequently than those with fewer college hours. This can be attributed to their superior understanding of criminal justice procedures, stronger communication skills, and enhanced problem-solving abilities, all of which make them valuable assets to their departments. In contrast, officers with fewer college hours were less likely to receive commendations or promotions. Truxillo et al. (1998) found that these officers were often confined to entry-level or patrol positions, with fewer opportunities for advancement. Citizen reviews of officers with higher education levels were generally more positive, reflecting the public's trust in their ability to manage situations with professionalism and fairness.

Education also plays a role in the likelihood of officers facing disciplinary actions. Officers with higher education levels—especially those with bachelor's degrees or higher—were less likely to face disciplinary actions. Truxillo et al. (1998) pointed out that these officers had a stronger understanding of departmental policies and legal regulations, making them less likely to violate protocol. Conversely, officers with limited college credits were more frequently involved in disciplinary actions, likely due to their lower comprehension of complex legal standards and ethical issues.

Hot-headed officers who act impulsively without fully understanding the implications of their actions are also more likely to face disciplinary actions, regardless of their level of education. This is because their lack of impulse control can lead to poor decision-making and potentially harmful consequences.

Disciplinary actions for officers with limited college credits may also stem from a lack of critical thinking skills and problem-solving abilities, which are often developed through higher education. Officers who receive ongoing training and education in areas such as conflict resolution and de-escalation techniques may be better equipped to handle challenging situations without resorting to disciplinary actions. This can lead to more positive outcomes and better community relationships. Of course, it's the intention of law enforcement agencies to ensure the safety and well-being of the community, and investing in the education and training of officers is crucial in achieving this goal. By providing opportunities for continuous learning, agencies can help officers make informed decisions and effectively navigate complex situations, ultimately leading to a more effective and trusted police force. The Turkish National Police, for example, has implemented a variety of training programs focused on de-escalation techniques and cultural competency to improve community relations. This proactive approach has been successful in reducing instances of violence and improving public trust in law enforcement. It is often during these critical moments that the training and skills acquired by officers are put to the test, emphasizing the importance of ongoing education and development in law enforcement. Investing in training programs can also help prevent unnecessary use of force and enhance overall officer safety.

Self-reports from officers with various education levels further illustrate this point. According to Beyhan (2008), officers with many college credits or advanced degrees often reported feeling more confident and prepared in their roles. They cited their education as a key factor in their ability to make sound decisions under pressure and to handle the intricacies of modern policing. In contrast, officers with limited college hours tended to report lower levels of job satisfaction and confidence, which were linked to their perceived lack of preparedness for more complex policing tasks.

The Turkish National Police converted its 9-month Police Training Schools to 2-year college degree programs in 2001 in their pursuit to improve the quality of police officers' job performance, police job preparedness levels, and the police service as a whole. It's no surprise that officers who receive more education tend to perform better. This is why many police departments are now requiring applicants to have a college degree.

As you have read, the relationship between education and job performance is one of the most critical aspects of modern policing. As noted by Leedy and Ormrod (2005), correlational research can provide valuable insights into how these two variables interact. In this case, officers with more education generally outperform those with less education, both in terms of technical skills and soft skills like communication and conflict resolution. Officers with higher levels of education are better equipped to understand the communities they serve, make quick and sound decisions in difficult situations, and navigate the legal complexities of their roles.

The characteristics of the two specific groups of people—officers with limited education and those with advanced education—highlight the importance of ongoing learning in law enforcement. Truxillo et al. (1998) found that the officers who invested in their education were often more adaptable, open-minded, and forward-thinking. These qualities not only improve job performance but also create opportunities for officers to advance into leadership positions within their departments.

A 10-year plan for police officers, particularly one that emphasizes continued education, is an invaluable tool for career development and job performance. The research shows that officers with higher education levels are better prepared, receive more commendations, and face fewer disciplinary actions than their peers with fewer college hours. The correlational studies conducted by Leedy and Ormrod (2005), Beyhan (2008), and Truxillo et al. (1998) provide strong evidence that investing in education pays off in the long run, both for individual officers and for the departments they serve. By understanding the importance of a 10-year plan and the relationship between education and performance, officers can set themselves up for success and ultimately provide better service to their communities.

Several studies have provided statistical insights into the relationship between education and promotions in law enforcement. Research consistently shows that officers with higher education levels—particularly those with bachelor's degrees or more advanced education—are more likely to receive promotions compared to their peers with less education. Here are a few relevant statistics and findings:

1. Truxillo et al. (1998) study found that officers with bachelor's degrees were promoted at a rate nearly 50% higher than officers with only a high school diploma. The study also noted that those with college credits beyond a bachelor's degree had an even higher likelihood of being promoted to leadership or specialized roles within their departments.

2. According to a Police Executive Research Forum (PERF) report, departments that require or encourage higher education see a correlation between education and promotions. For example, officers with college degrees tend to be promoted quicker to sergeant, lieutenant, and captain positions than those without degrees. 58% of police chiefs surveyed stated that officers with a bachelor's degree or higher were more likely to be promoted faster than those without.

3. The National Center for Education Statistics (NCES) published data indicating that law enforcement officers with at least a bachelor's degree were 87% more likely to be promoted to supervisory positions within their first 10 years on the force, compared to those without any post-secondary education. This was attributed to the officers' improved decision-making skills, leadership potential, and understanding of complex legal issues.

4. Beyhan's (2008) study of Turkish police officers found similar trends, showing that officers with higher education, particularly those with bachelor's degrees or higher, were more likely to be promoted within their departments. Officers with post-graduate education were often targeted for leadership and administrative positions.

These statistics consistently demonstrate that education is a significant factor in determining promotion rates within law enforcement. The data suggests that officers with higher levels of education not only perform better in their roles but also advance quicker through the ranks, securing leadership and specialized positions at a much faster rate than their less-educated counterparts.

Several studies and reports provide data on the relationship between education levels and the likelihood of police officers receiving commendations. Commendations, which are formal recognitions for outstanding job performance or service, tend to be awarded more frequently to officers with higher education levels. Here are some key findings on this topic:

1. Truxillo et al. (1998) found that officers with bachelor's degrees or higher received more commendations than officers with less education. In this 10-year longitudinal study, officers with higher education were 30% more likely to receive commendations for exemplary performance, teamwork, and leadership compared to those with only a high school diploma. The study suggested that the improved critical thinking, communication skills, and problem-solving abilities that come with higher education contributed to these officers excelling in complex situations that often led to commendations.

2. Police Executive Research Forum (PERF) also found a positive correlation between higher education and receiving commendations. In departments where education was valued, officers with a college degree were awarded commendations at a rate 25–40% higher than

those without a degree. The commendations often reflected the officers' contributions in areas such as community policing, de-escalation, and conflict resolution, areas where advanced education is believed to have a significant impact.

3. Beyhan (2008), in his study of Turkish police officers, found that officers with bachelor's and master's degrees were more likely to receive both internal and public commendations. Officers with higher education received 20% more commendations for acts of bravery, leadership in critical incidents, and community outreach compared to their peers with only basic education or fewer college credits.

4. U.S. Department of Justice (DOJ) reports have similarly found that officers with at least some college education were more likely to receive commendations related to community service, ethical policing, and professionalism. The DOJ data showed that officers with a four-year degree were 40% more likely to be recognized for their ability to handle complex or high-pressure situations effectively, leading to commendations from both peers and community members.

These findings suggest that education not only enhances an officer's technical and procedural knowledge but also positively impacts their ability to perform in a way that earns recognition. Officers with higher education tend to receive more commendations, which are indicators of their competence, professionalism, and leadership in the field.

CHAPTER 07

THEORETICAL FRAMEWORKS IN EDUCATION AND POLICING

Education and policing are intertwined in shaping well-rounded, socially responsible individuals prepared to address complex societal issues. Three key theoretical frameworks underpin the relationship between education and the preparation of police officers: Liberal Education Theory, the Integrative Model, and the Theory of Cognitive Development. Liberal Education Theory emphasizes the importance of a broad, interdisciplinary education that promotes critical thinking and problem-solving skills. The Integrative Model focuses on the integration of academic knowledge with practical skills to prepare police officers for real-world challenges. The theory of Cognitive Development highlights the importance of understanding how individuals learn and develop their thinking processes in order to effectively educate and train future law enforcement professionals.

Liberal Education Theory posits that education extends beyond academics, emphasizing the development of social responsibility. This approach is critical in policing, encouraging future law enforcement officers to engage with and uphold societal values, thus playing a significant role in their communities. By incorporating both Cognitive Development and Liberal Education Theory into police training programs, officers are better equipped to handle complex situations with critical thinking skills and a strong sense of ethical responsibility. This comprehensive approach ensures that law enforcement professionals are not only knowledgeable in their field but also committed to serving and protecting their communities with integrity. As Conrad once stated, "society demands good conduct and responsibility from those who enforce the law." By instilling these values in future law enforcement officers, we can create a more just and ethical society where everyone feels safe and protected." Conrad, C., & Wyer, J. C. (1980). Liberal education in transition. Washington, D.C.: American Association for Higher Education.

The Integrative Model, as suggested by Conrad and Wyer (1980), illustrates how universities have evolved their curricula to include broader social and environmental concerns, promoting a more holistic approach to education. This model emphasizes a core subject structure that helps students connect academic learning with real-world issues, making it particularly relevant to the field of policing. In this way, the Integrative Model not only prepares students for their future careers but also instills a sense of responsibility and ethical awareness in them. By incorporating these broader concerns into the curriculum, universities are contributing to the development of a more ethical society where everyone feels safe and protected.

Police officers trained under this model are not only equipped with the necessary skills and knowledge to handle various situations effectively but also understand the importance of upholding ethical standards and serving their communities with integrity. This comprehensive approach to education ultimately benefits society as a whole by producing well-rounded professionals who are committed to promoting justice and safety.

The Theory of Cognitive Development highlights the role of higher education in enhancing students' intellectual abilities. According to Gurin, Dey, Hurtado, and Gurin (2002), institutions cultivate students' cognitive skills, enabling them to process complex information and adapt effectively to changing environments. This development is essential for police officers, as they must navigate a variety of challenging and unpredictable situations.

These frameworks collectively underscore the importance of education in preparing individuals for the multifaceted demands of policing, ensuring they are equipped not only with technical knowledge but also with the social and cognitive skills necessary for their role.

WORKING EXAMPLES OF THEORETICAL FRAMEWORKS IN LAW ENFORCEMENT EDUCATION

Liberal Education Theory focuses on creating social responsibility, critical thinking, and ethical decision-making. In practice, law enforcement officers trained under this framework would be equipped to handle complex social issues, such as community relations and conflict resolution. For example, an officer responding to a protest would not only enforce the law but also consider the broader social context—listening to grievances, de-escalating tensions, and respecting the rights of individuals to peacefully assemble.

This approach protects both the officers and the public by reducing the likelihood of violent confrontations and advocating trust between law enforcement and the community. By instilling a strong sense of ethics and social responsibility, officers are less likely to engage in excessive use of force, protecting their own well-being and the public's safety. This, in turn, promotes a safer environment for all parties involved and strengthens community trust in law enforcement, which can lead to more effective policing over time.

The Integrative Model suggests combining different academic disciplines and social issues to create a well-rounded education. For example, law enforcement officers could benefit from coursework that integrates psychology, sociology, and criminal justice, allowing them to better understand human behavior, mental health issues, and social inequalities.

An officer responding to a domestic violence situation, for instance, could draw from both their knowledge of the law and their understanding of psychological trauma to handle the situation with empathy and professionalism.

By incorporating a broader curriculum into law enforcement training, officers are more prepared to handle the wide variety of situations they may encounter on the job. This holistic training protects both officers and the public by equipping officers with the tools to de-escalate situations, communicate effectively, and resolve conflicts without resorting to violence. In turn, this helps keep officers safer in high-stress situations and reduces the risk of harm to the public.

The Theory of Cognitive Development emphasizes the importance of critical thinking, problem-solving, and adapting to new situations. Law enforcement officers trained with this theory in mind are better prepared to think on their feet and make sound decisions in dynamic and often high-pressure situations. For example, an officer responding to an active shooter scenario would need to quickly assess the situation, weigh the risks, and determine the best course of action to protect themselves and the public.

Cognitive development allows officers to process complex information rapidly and effectively.

By fostering these cognitive skills, officers are better equipped to make decisions that prioritize both their safety and that of the public. For instance, officers can assess the most strategic way to enter a dangerous situation, minimizing risk to themselves while working to neutralize the threat. This not only enhances the officers' safety but also maximizes the chances of protecting civilians from harm.

Incorporating Liberal Education Theory, the Integrative Model, and the Theory of Cognitive Development into law enforcement training ensures that officers are not only skilled in law enforcement tactics but also socially responsible, ethically grounded, and cognitively prepared to handle complex situations. These educational frameworks help officers protect and serve the public more effectively while ensuring their own safety. The ultimate goal is to create a law enforcement system where officers are well-equipped to handle the diverse challenges of modern policing, ensuring a safer society for everyone involved.

Liberal Education Theory emphasizes that education is more than academic knowledge; it fosters the development of social responsibility and ethical thinking. According to Conrad and Wyer (1980), liberal education aims to cultivate well-rounded individuals who are equipped to contribute to society in meaningful ways. This theory underscores the importance of preparing students to engage in critical thinking, ethical reasoning, and active participation in their communities.

For future law enforcement officers, these values are essential, as policing involves more than enforcing laws—it involves serving and protecting the community while upholding justice and fairness. Every community, whether it is urban or rural, faces unique challenges and requires law enforcement officers who are not only knowledgeable about the law but also possess strong ethical principles and a commitment to serving the public good. Therefore, incorporating liberal education principles into law enforcement training can help develop officers who are better equipped to navigate complex situations with integrity and compassion.

In the context of policing, liberal education can help law enforcement officers approach their roles with a broader understanding of social issues and a deeper sense of civic duty. By instilling these values, officers can better understand the communities they serve, respect diverse perspectives, and approach their duties with a mindset geared toward ethical behavior and social justice. This perspective moves beyond a narrow focus on law enforcement as merely a technical task and encourages officers to view themselves as public servants who play a critical role in shaping a just and equitable society. When it comes to addressing complex issues such as systemic racism, poverty, and mental health, a liberal education can provide officers with the critical thinking skills and empathy necessary to navigate these challenges effectively. Ultimately, integrating liberal education into law enforcement training can lead to more compassionate and effective policing practices that prioritize community well-being and social justice. There are so many neighborhoods and even cities where officers are needed to not only enforce the law but also build trust and relationships with the community. By incorporating liberal education into their training, officers can better understand the diverse perspectives and experiences of the people they serve, ultimately creating a more inclusive and responsive approach to policing.

Conrad and Wyer (1980) argue that a liberal education approach is transformative because it equips students with the tools to analyze complex societal issues and develop informed responses. In the field of policing, this is particularly valuable because officers are frequently called upon to navigate intricate social dynamics and make split-second decisions that can have far-reaching consequences. A liberal education can provide the ethical foundation necessary to make sound, just decisions in these moments.

The Integrative Model, as proposed by Conrad and Wyer (1980), suggests that higher education institutions should foster interdisciplinary learning by connecting different parts of the curriculum.

This model emphasizes the importance of a holistic approach to education, where students are exposed to a wide range of subjects and are encouraged to make connections between them. In this framework, a university curriculum might integrate courses on social justice, environmental issues, and other contemporary concerns, which can be tied back to the core subject of policing. It can also include experiential learning opportunities, such as internships or service-learning projects, to further enhance students' understanding of how different disciplines intersect in real-world contexts. This approach not only prepares students for a diverse and interconnected world but also encourages critical thinking and problem-solving skills essential for addressing complex societal issues.

As time goes on and the needs of the community change, the area of study might evolve to incorporate new technologies and methodologies in policing, ensuring that students are equipped with the most up-to-date knowledge and skills. Collaboration with professionals in the field can provide valuable insights and networking opportunities for students pursuing careers in law enforcement or related fields.

This integrative approach is particularly relevant for law enforcement education, as policing is a multifaceted profession that intersects with various social, legal, and ethical concerns. By exposing students to a broad curriculum that includes topics such as sociology, psychology, ethics, and environmental studies, the Integrative Model prepares future officers to engage with the complexities of the modern world. For example, courses on social justice issues can help law enforcement officers understand systemic inequalities and develop more empathetic and informed responses when interacting with marginalized communities. The psychology courses can provide insights into human behavior and decision-making, helping officers de-escalate tense situations and build trust with individuals in crisis. Overall, the Integrative Model aims to cultivate well-rounded and socially conscious law enforcement professionals who are equipped to navigate the challenges of policing in today's society.

The core of the Integrative Model lies in its ability to cluster educational experiences around a central theme, creating a more interconnected and meaningful learning process for students. Conrad and Wyer (1980) highlight how this method fosters a more comprehensive educational experience, allowing students to see the broader social implications of their work. In policing, this means that officers are not just learning technical skills in isolation but are also developing an awareness of the broader social and environmental context in which they operate. This prepares them to address contemporary challenges with a well-rounded, informed perspective.

The Theory of Cognitive Development, as discussed by Gurin, Dey, Hurtado, and Gurin (2002), focuses on the role of higher education in enhancing students' intellectual and cognitive abilities. This theory suggests that institutions of higher learning help students develop the capacity to process complex information, think critically, and adapt to changing environments. In the context of policing, these skills are crucial, as officers often face unpredictable situations that require quick thinking and problem-solving. When officers are equipped to think critically and adapt to changing environments, they are better able to assess situations effectively and make informed decisions that promote public safety. This highlights the importance of incorporating cognitive development theories into police training programs to enhance officers' abilities to navigate challenging and dynamic situations. Every situation could be different, and having a strong foundation in cognitive development can help officers approach each scenario with a clear and analytical mindset. By understanding how individuals process information and make decisions, officers can better anticipate potential outcomes and respond appropriately in high-pressure situations.

Going from one area to the next, officers must be able to adapt quickly and effectively to ensure the safety of themselves and others. Incorporating cognitive development theories into training programs can provide officers with the tools they need to make split-second decisions that can ultimately save lives. Saving themselves is crucial so that other lives can ultimately be saved as well. This level of cognitive training can also help officers de-escalate tense situations and minimize the use of force when necessary. By continuously honing their cognitive skills, law enforcement officers can better serve and protect their communities. The ultimate goal is for everyone to be safe and for conflicts to be resolved peacefully. This approach can help build trust between law enforcement and the communities they serve, leading to a safer and more cohesive society overall.

Gurin et al. (2002) argue that the cognitive development of students is a key outcome of higher education. Law enforcement officers must be able to handle complex situations, such as de-escalating conflicts, analyzing evidence, and making split-second decisions under pressure. Higher education institutions, by promoting cognitive development, prepare students to manage these challenges more effectively. The ability to process more complex information, adapt to new circumstances, and approach problems from multiple perspectives is essential for law enforcement officers who must operate in dynamic environments. It is during these times that the critical thinking skills and analytical abilities learned during higher education prove invaluable in ensuring public safety and upholding the law. By pursuing a deeper understanding of societal issues and ethical considerations, higher education equips future law enforcement officers with the tools needed to navigate the complexities of their roles with professionalism and integrity.

Morgan, Morgan, Foster, and Kolbert (2000) suggest that the development of personality traits, such as moral reasoning and ethical decision-making, occurs during early adulthood. As a result, higher education institutions play a critical role in shaping the moral and ethical foundation of future law enforcement officers. According to Morgan et al. (2000), education can promote the moral and conceptual development of law enforcement trainees, helping them to become more thoughtful, empathetic, and responsible public servants. It isn't how a person might have been brought up but rather the education and training they receive that ultimately shapes their ethical decision-making abilities in the field of law enforcement. This highlights the importance of continuous education and professional development programs for law enforcement officers to ensure they uphold the highest standards of integrity throughout their careers.

Changing one's mindset and expanding their knowledge base through ongoing learning opportunities can lead to improved ethical decision-making and behavior in the complex and challenging situations law enforcement officers often face. By prioritizing continuous education, agencies can cultivate a culture of accountability and ethical conduct within their ranks, ultimately benefiting both officers and the communities they serve.

This theoretical framework emphasizes that law enforcement officers are not only shaped by the technical aspects of their training but also by their ability to engage in complex cognitive processes. The development of critical thinking, ethical reasoning, and the capacity to navigate changing environments is vital for effective policing. Cognitive development in higher education provides officers with the mental tools they need to succeed in a demanding and often unpredictable profession.

Being equipped with strong critical thinking skills allows officers to make informed decisions in high-pressure situations, leading to better outcomes for both themselves and the public. Ethical reasoning helps officers uphold the values of justice and fairness in their interactions with the community, fostering trust and cooperation. For officers to go home to their families each night, it is essential that they have the ability to navigate complex ethical dilemmas with integrity and empathy. By integrating cognitive development and ethical reasoning into police training programs, law enforcement agencies can better prepare their officers to handle the challenges they may face on the job.

The Liberal Education Theory, the Integrative Model, and the Theory of Cognitive Development each offer valuable insights into how education can shape future law enforcement officers. Liberal Education Theory emphasizes the importance of social responsibility and ethical thinking, while the Integrative Model highlights the need for a broad, interdisciplinary approach to learning that connects various aspects of the curriculum. The Theory of Cognitive Development underscores the role of higher education in cultivating critical thinking, problem-solving, and moral reasoning.

Together, these frameworks provide a comprehensive approach to law enforcement education, ensuring that future officers are not only technically proficient but also socially and ethically grounded. By incorporating these educational theories into law enforcement training, institutions can help create a more just and ethical society where law enforcement officers are better equipped to serve and protect their communities.

Citations

Then and Now on Policing

Walker, S., & Katz, C. M. (2012). The Police in America: An Introduction. McGraw-Hill Education.

Peak, K. J., & Glensor, R. W. (2002). Community Policing and Problem Solving: Strategies and Practices. Prentice Hall.

Potter, G. (2013). The History of Policing in the United States, Part 1. Eastern Kentucky University.

Carter, D. L. (1995). Police Use of Force: Official Reports, Citizen Complaints, and Legal Consequences. National Institute of Justice.

Department of Justice (DOJ). (1990). The Comprehensive Report of the Wickersham Commission on Law Observance and Enforcement. Washington, DC: U.S. Government Printing Office.

Finckenauer, J. O. (2005). Professionalizing the Police. U.S. Department of Justice, Office of Justice Programs.

Finnegan, R. (1976). The Impact of Higher Education on Police Performance. Journal of Criminal Justice, 4(1), 67-75.

Stevens, D. J. (2017). Policing and Community Partnership: A Guide to Engaging the Community and Building Trust.

POLICING FROM THE 1960S TO NOW

1. Civil Rights Movement and Policing Reforms

During the 1960s and 1970s, the Civil Rights Movement demanded greater accountability for law enforcement, especially in regard to the treatment of African Americans and other marginalized groups. This period saw the establishment of Miranda Rights in 1966, ensuring suspects were informed of their legal rights.

2. Impact of the War on Drugs

The War on Drugs, initiated by President Richard Nixon in the 1970s, focused on the criminalization of drug use and distribution, resulting in increased law enforcement efforts and militarized responses. This era contributed to mass incarceration, disproportionately affecting minority communities.

3. Community Policing

The introduction of community policing in the 1990s marked a shift from punitive measures to building relationships between officers and communities to reduce crime through preventive strategies.

4. Technological Advancements in Policing

In the 2000s, technological advancements, including body cameras and predictive policing algorithms, transformed law enforcement practices, increasing transparency and accountability while sparking debates on privacy and surveillance.

5. Modern Policing Incentives

Salaries in policing increased significantly by 2023, with states like California offering higher wages and generous pensions. Defined benefit pension plans remain a critical incentive for officers.

6. International Comparisons

In the United States, officers are equipped with military-grade equipment, while the United Kingdom emphasizes de-escalation techniques and less-lethal options. Public scrutiny and union influence also differ significantly between the two countries.

State the Facts, Ma'am: The Importance of Evidence-Based Policing Over Intuition

1. Lawrence Sherman - The creator of the Evidence-Based Policing (EBP) methodology, emphasizing the use of empirical evidence to guide policing strategies, policies, and practices.

2. Operation Ceasefire - A notable example of evidence-based policing, implemented in Boston in the mid-1990s to reduce gun violence through data analysis and targeted interventions.

3. Problem-Oriented Policing in Newport News - A case where the Newport News Police Department applied evidence-based strategies to address burglary in public housing, resulting in a significant reduction in crime.

4. Randomized Control Trials in Stop-and-Search Operations - Research demonstrating the effectiveness of data-driven approaches in reducing racial disparities in policing.

5. Body-Worn Cameras (BWCs) - Mentioned as an evidence-based tool that promotes accountability and transparency, with research supporting its role in reducing the use of force and complaints against officers.

6. Predictive Policing - Uses algorithms and data analysis to forecast potential criminal activity, allowing for proactive resource allocation.

7. Crime Mapping and Geographic Information Systems (GIS) - Highlighted as tools enabling law enforcement to visualize crime patterns and deploy resources effectively.

8. Cognitive Biases - References common biases in intuitive policing, such as confirmation bias, availability heuristic, and anchoring bias, which impact decision-making.

9. Wrongful Convictions - Discusses the personal, legal, and economic consequences for individuals wrongfully convicted due to assumption-based policing.

10. Training and Education - Advocated as a solution to improve officer decision-making, reduce bias, and enhance evidence-based practices in law enforcement.

HISTORICAL MOVEMENTS AND INCENTIVES IN POLICING (1960S TO THE 2000S)

Academic Journals

1. Walker, S. (2005). The New World of Police Accountability. Crime and Justice, 34(1), 451-482. Focuses on the impact of civil rights movements and federal legislation on police practices.

2. Reiss, A. J. (1971). Police Brutality—Answers to Key Questions. Annals of the American Academy of Political and Social Science, 374(1), 1-10. Examines early critiques of policing practices during the 1960s and the role of public oversight.

3. Kraska, P. B. (2007). Militarization and Policing—Its Relevance to 21st Century Police. Policing: A Journal of Policy and Practice, 1(4), 501-513. Discusses the militarization of police forces post-9/11.

4. Mauer, M. (1999). The Impact of Mandatory Minimum Penalties in Federal Sentencing. Federal Sentencing Reporter, 12(2), 3-9. Covers how the War on Drugs influenced policing incentives and practices.

GOVERNMENT REPORTS

1. President's Commission on Law Enforcement and Administration of Justice (1967). The Challenge of Crime in a Free Society. A foundational report examining crime and policing challenges in the 1960s.

2. Bureau of Justice Statistics (1994). Violent Crime Control and Law Enforcement Act of 1994: Summary and Analysis. Details the largest crime bill in U.S. history and its implications for policing incentives.

3. National Institute of Justice (1998). Broken Windows and Police Discretion. Discusses the implementation of broken windows theory in law enforcement practices.

4. U.S. Department of Justice (2006). Policing in the Post-9/11 Era. Explores the shift in law enforcement strategies following the September 11, 2001, attacks.

HISTORICAL COURT DECISIONS

1. Miranda v. Arizona, 384 U.S. 436 (1966). Established the requirement for police to inform suspects of their rights, reflecting broader concerns about police accountability.

2. Terry v. Ohio, 392 U.S. 1 (1968). Legalized stop-and-frisk tactics under specific conditions, impacting policing practices.

3. United States v. Leon, 468 U.S. 897 (1984). Introduced the "good faith" exception to the exclusionary rule, influencing police search practices.

4. Whren v. United States, 517 U.S. 806 (1996). Upheld the use of pretextual traffic stops, shaping policing and racial profiling debates.

BOOKS AND PUBLICATIONS

1. Balko, R. (2013). Rise of the Warrior Cop: The Militarization of America's Police Forces. Public Affairs. Comprehensive history of the militarization of police forces from the 1960s onward.

2. Vitale, A. (2017). The End of Policing. Verso. Critiques modern policing practices and provides a historical overview of systemic issues.

3. Kelling, G. L., & Wilson, J. Q. (1982). Broken Windows: The Police and Neighborhood Safety. The Atlantic Monthly. Introduces the "broken windows theory" that influenced community policing practices.

4. Hinton, E. (2016). From the War on Poverty to the War on Crime: The Making of Mass Incarceration in America. Harvard University Press. Examines how federal policies in the 1960s and beyond transformed policing and criminal justice.

5. Walker, S., & Katz, C. M. (2011). The Police in America: An Introduction. McGraw-Hill Education. A textbook offering a thorough history of policing in the U.S.

Military Experience and Policing

1. Walker, A. (2010)

This source is cited multiple times in the chapter, particularly in relation to employment rates between veterans and non-veterans. Walker's research highlights the adaptability and relevance of military skills in civilian roles, such as law enforcement.

2. Specific Studies or Articles on Military Transition

While not directly cited in the excerpt, references to the transferable skills, challenges, and strengths of veterans suggest a reliance on broader studies or government reports about military transitions to civilian jobs and their application in law enforcement.

3. Key Concepts on Leadership and Communication

General military and leadership training manuals, as well as academic studies on the transition from military to civilian life, may provide additional foundational support. For instance, works focusing on the relationship between structured military environments and similar structures in policing.

4. Mental Health in Veterans

The discussion on the mental health challenges veterans face implies familiarity with reports or studies from organizations such as the National Institute of Mental Health (NIMH), Veterans Affairs (VA), or journals like the Journal of Traumatic Stress.

THE EXAMINATION OF VIABLE RESEARCH BETWEEN TURKISH AND US POLICE OFFICERS

Leedy & Ormrod (2005): "Correlational research design is appropriate for studies gathering data on two or more characteristics of a group, allowing researchers to examine relationships between variables."

Beyhan (2008): "The impact of higher education on job preparedness was significant, especially among officers with bachelor's degrees or higher, although performance metrics based on self-reports can be inflated."

Truxillo et al. (1998): "A longitudinal study over 10 years allows for the analysis of promotions, disciplinary actions, and educational advancements during an officer's career. Officers with higher education levels were less likely to face disciplinary actions."

HISTORICAL MOVEMENTS AND INCENTIVES (1960s–2000s)

1. Miranda Rights (1966)

Miranda v. Arizona, 384 U.S. 436 (1966). Supreme Court of the United States.

National Archives, "Miranda v. Arizona (1966)."

https://www.archives.gov/milestone-documents/miranda-v-arizona

2. War on Drugs

President Nixon's Special Message to the Congress on Drug Abuse Prevention and Control, June 17, 1971. The American Presidency Project. https://www.presidency.ucsb.edu/documents/special-message-the-congress-drug-abuse-prevention-and-control

Drug Policy Alliance, "A Brief History of the Drug War." https://drugpolicy.org/issues/brief-history-drug-war

3. Community Policing

U.S. Department of Justice, Office of Community Oriented Policing Services (COPS Office). https://cops.usdoj.gov/

4. Changes from the 1960s to Today

Police Salaries and Benefits

Bureau of Labor Statistics, U.S. Department of Labor, Occupational Outlook Handbook, "Police and Detectives."

https://www.bls.gov/ooh/protective-service/police-and-detectives.htm

5. Police Unions

Walker, S., & Katz, C. M. (2013). "The Police in America: An Introduction." New York: McGraw-Hill Education.

DIFFERENCES BETWEEN STATES IN THE U.S.

California Police Salaries

California Employment Development Department, "Occupational Employment and Wages." https://www.labormarketinfo.edd.ca.gov/

Texas and Florida Police Unions

Combined Law Enforcement Associations of Texas (CLEAT). https://www.cleat.org/

Florida Police Benevolent Association (FPBA). https://www.flpba.org/

Variations Between Countries

United States vs. United Kingdom policing

College of Policing, "Training and Development." https://www.college.police.uk/

Bureau of Labor Statistics, U.S. Department of Labor, "Occupational Outlook Handbook: Police and Detectives." https://www.bls.gov/ooh/protective-service/police-and-detectives.htm

Community Policing and Public Perception

Community policing in the UK

College of Policing, "Community Policing."
https://www.college.police.uk/guidance/community-policing

Public Perception and Technology in Policing

U.S. Department of Justice, Office of Community Oriented Policing Services
(COPS Office). https://cops.usdoj.gov/

Police Executive Research Forum (PERF), "Use of Technology in Policing."
https://www.policeforum.org/

General Sources for Trends and Changes in Policing

THE BLACK LIVES MATTER MOVEMENT

Black Lives Matter, "About." https://blacklivesmatter.com/about/

Legislative Reforms

Congressional Research Service, "Police Reform and the 116th Congress: Selected Legal Issues."
https://crsreports.congress.gov/product/pdf/R/R46530

Conrad, C. & Wyer, J. C. (1980). Liberal education in transition. Washington, D.C.: American Association for Higher Education.

Gurin, P., Dey, E. L., Hurtado, S., & Gurin, G. (2002). Diversity and higher education: Theory and impact on educational outcomes. Harvard Educational Review, 72(3), 330-366. Retrieved from www.temple.edu/tlc/resources/handouts/diversity/gurin_and_hurtado.pdf

Morgan, B., Morgan, F., Foster, V., & Kolbert, J. (2000). Promoting the moral and conceptual development of law enforcement trainees: A deliberate psychological educational approach. Journal of Moral Education, 29(2), 203-218.

THEORETICAL FRAMEWORKS IN EDUCATION AND POLICING

1. Conrad, C., & Wyer, J. C. (1980). Liberal education in transition. Washington, D.C.: American Association for Higher Education.

2. The Integrative Model, Conrad and Wyer (1980), illustrates how universities have evolved their curricula to include broader social and environmental concerns, promoting a more holistic approach to education.

3. Conrad and Wyer (1980) state that liberal education aims to cultivate well-rounded individuals who are equipped to contribute to society in meaningful ways.

4. Conrad and Wyer (1980) argue that a liberal education approach is transformative because it equips students with the tools to analyze complex societal issues and develop informed responses.

5. The Integrative Model, as proposed by Conrad and Wyer (1980), suggests that higher education institutions should foster interdisciplinary learning by connecting different parts of the curriculum.

6. The Theory of Cognitive Development highlights the role of higher education in enhancing students' intellectual abilities. According to Gurin, Dey, Hurtado, and Gurin (2002).

7. The Theory of Cognitive Development, as discussed by Gurin, Dey, Hurtado, and Gurin (2002), focuses on the role of higher education in enhancing students' intellectual and cognitive abilities.

8. Gurin et al. (2002) argue that the cognitive development of students is a key outcome of higher education.

9. Morgan, Morgan, Foster, and Kolbert (2000) suggest that the development of personality traits, such as moral reasoning and ethical decision-making, occurs during early adulthood.

Historical Movements and Incentives (1960s-2000s)

1. Miranda Rights (1966)

Miranda v. Arizona, 384 U.S. 436 (1966). Supreme Court of the United States.

National Archives, Miranda v. Arizona (1966)

https://www.archives.gov/milestone-documents/miranda-v-arizona

2. War on Drugs

President Nixon Special Message to the Congress on Drug Abuse Prevention and

Control, June 17, 1971. The American Presidency Project.

https://www.presidency.ucsb.edu/documents/special-message-the-congress-drug-abuse-prevention-and-control

Drug Policy Alliance A Brief History of the Drug War

https://drugpolicy.org/issues/brief-history-drug-war

3. Community Policing

U.S. Department of Justice, Office of Community Oriented Policing Services (COPS Office). https://cops.usdoj.gov/

Changes from the 1960s to Today

1. Police Salaries and Benefits

Bureau of Labor Statistics, U.S. Department of Labor, Occupational Outlook Handbook,

Police and Detectives

https://www.bls.gov/ooh/protective-service/police-and-detectives.htm

2. Police Unions

Walker, S., Katz, C. M. (2013) The Police in America: An Introduction New York: McGraw-Hill Education.

Differences Between States in the U.S.

1. California Police Salaries

California Employment Development Department, Occupational Employment and Wages

https://www.labormarketinfo.edd.ca.gov/

2. Texas and Florida Police Unions

Combined Law Enforcement Associations of Texas (CLEAT). https://www.cleat.org/

Florida Police Benevolent Association (FPBA). https://www.flpba.org/

Variations Between Countries

1. United States vs. United Kingdom Policing

College of Policing, Training and Development

https://www.college.police.uk/

Bureau of Labor Statistics, U.S. Department of Labor, Occupational Outlook Handbook:

Police and Detectives

https://www.bls.gov/ooh/protective-service/police-and-detectives.htm

Community Policing and Public Perception

1. Community Policing in the UK

College of Policing, Community Policing

https://www.college.police.uk/guidance/community-policing

2. Public Perception and Technology in Policing

U.S. Department of Justice, Office of Community Oriented Policing Services (COPS Office). https://cops.usdoj.gov/

Police Executive Research Forum (PERF), Use of Technology in Policing

https://www.policeforum.org/

General Sources for Trends and Changes in Policing

1. Black Lives Matter Movement

https://blacklivesmatter.com/about/

2. Legislative Reforms

Congressional Research Service, Police Reform and the 116th Congress: Selected

Legal Issues https://crsreports.congress.gov/product/pdf/R/R46530

The Wickersham Crime Commission (1931) was among the first of several groups to recommend higher educational standards for law enforcement officers.

ABOUT THE AUTHOR

DR. WINSTON HARRIS is a current Professor of Higher Education and a retired police officer and detective with a distinguished career spanning 23 years. Rising through the ranks from Park Police to Detective, Sergeant, 1st Sergeant, and eventually Captain in the South/West Division, Dr. Harris displayed unwavering dedication to public service and community engagement.

While serving as a detective, Dr. Harris demonstrated expertise in selective enforcement and drug unit operations. In leadership roles, they championed community outreach by creating events like an essay contest titled "Why I Did Not Join a Gang" and organizing Chats with the Commander meetings to encourage dialogue with local residents.

A strong advocate for personal and professional development, Dr. Harris pursued higher education with support from their police department, earning a master's degree in General Administration and, in April 2014, a Ph.D. in Criminal Justice from Capella University. The achievements of Dr. Harris were further enriched by active participation in the Police Athletics/Activities League as a board member.

The benefits offered by their police department, including tuition assistance, paid time for college courses, degree incentives, and salary enhancements, played a crucial role in their upward mobility. Today, Dr. Harris combines extensive field experience with academic expertise to inspire and educate future leaders in the field of higher education.

Dr. Winston Harris is a dedicated military veteran who began his career in the U.S. Army, where he received a wealth of knowledge and skills serving the nation. After completing his service in the Army, Harris transitioned to the Air Force Reserve, where he continued to contribute to the United States national defense. Over the course of 24 years in the Reserve, Harris demonstrated unwavering dedication and professionalism, ultimately retiring with a wealth of experience and a deep sense of pride in his service.

www.ingramcontent.com/pod-product-compliance
Lightning Source LLC
Chambersburg PA
CBHW051221120626
46547CB00013B/1458